SANYO

Microwave Cooking

A Benjamin Company Book

Editor: Julie Hogan
Production Managers: Pat Drew, Susan Jablonski, Virginia Schomp
Editorial Assistants: Greta Ebel, Jane Nawrocki
Director, Consumer Education & Services: Thelma Pressman
Chief Home Economist: Betty Sullivan
Consulting Home Economists: Carol Peterson, Paul Pressman
Art & Design: Thomas C. Brecklin
Photography: Teri Sandison
Typography: A-Line, Milwaukee

USER INSTRUCTIONS

PRECAUTIONS TO AVOID POSSIBLE EXPOSURE TO EXCESSIVE MICROWAVE ENERGY

(a) DO NOT ATTEMPT to operate this oven with the door open since open-door operation can result in harmful exposure to microwave energy. It is important not to defeat or tamper with the safety interlocks.

(b) DO NOT PLACE any object between the oven front face and the door or allow soil or cleaner residue to accumulate on sealing surfaces.

(c) DO NOT OPERATE the oven if it is damaged. It is particularly important that the oven door closes properly and that there is no damage to the:
  (1) DOOR (bent)
  (2) HINGES AND LATCHES (broken or loosened)
  (3) DOOR SEALS AND SEALING SURFACES

(d) THE OVEN SHOULD NOT BE ADJUSTED OR REPAIRED BY ANYONE EXCEPT PROPERLY QUALIFIED SERVICE PERSONNEL.

Library of Congress Catalog Card Number: 82-70711
ISBN: 0-87502-125-5
Published by The Benjamin Company, Inc.
One Westchester Plaza
Elmsford, New York 10523
Printed in Japan
10 9 8 7 6 5 4 3 2

Table of Contents

HOW DOES IT WORK?

Congratulations! You have now selected an exciting cooking appliance that can help you prepare delicious meals in minutes. We will do our part by showing you the way it works, why it works that way, what it can do, and how you can very quickly become an accomplished microwave cook. What you must do is take the time, as with any new appliance, to read the instructions carefully.

A COOKING SCHOOL

These illustrated introductory chapters are designed to be a cooking school in book form. There is nothing complicated about using a microwave oven; all you need is a little understanding of its special qualities and how it responds to food.

To install your microwave oven, follow the Use and Care Manual's directions. You will be pleased to learn your microwave requires little maintenance. Unlike a conventional oven which generates heat in the oven cavity, there is no heat in the microwave, so food and grease cannot bake on. Just a simple wiping is all it needs.

CONVENTIONAL COOKING VS MICROWAVE

In conventional top-of-the-range cooking by gas or electricity, food cooks by heat applied to the bottom of the pan. In a conventional oven, by hot air which first heats the oven cavity, then the food. In microwave cooking, no heat source is employed. Microwaves are directed to the food. This simple technology eliminates wasted energy. The energy is used only to cook the food, not to heat the air first. Inside the microwave is a magnetron vacuum tube that converts ordinary household electric current into high-frequency microwaves. As in radio and TV sets, these microwaves are designed to perform at a microwave frequency assigned by the FCC (Federal Communications Commission). In the oven, a stirrer-fan helps distribute the microwaves evenly throughout the oven cavity. Microwaves are either reflected, passed through, or absorbed, depending upon the material contacted. Metal reflects microwaves; glass, pottery, paper, and most plastics allow the microwaves to pass through; and, finally, food absorbs microwaves. The absorbed microwaves cause molecules in the food to vibrate rapidly against each other, producing friction and creating heat. This process is the same as when heat is generated when you rub your hands together. Cooking begins from the outside layer of the food and, by conduction, the interior of food cooks, just as it

Microwaves bounce off oven walls and are absorbed by food. The air in the oven remains cool.

does in a conventional oven. It just does it faster. Because cooking containers used in the microwave oven do not absorb microwave energy, they do not become hot unless the heat of the food itself eventually warms the dish. Depending upon the food and the design of the dish, there may be times, however, when you will need to use potholders. The see-through metal screen in the door reflects the microwaves, yet enables you to observe the food as it cooks. Opening the microwave oven door turns the unit off automatically so you can stir, turn, or check doneness with ease. The removable glass tray helps to elevate the food for even cooking. And all of this with the bonus of an easy-to-clean, cool cavity.

Before we go to cooking school, the next chapter introduces us to just a few of the reasons why it will be an enjoyable and tasty education.

Conventional oven cooks by hot air.

WHAT IT DOES BEST

You can cook just about anything in the microwave oven, but some food is so especially good done this way that we want to show several of them to you. Let's take a look.

□ *Roast beef* is juicy and rare, with less shrinkage than in the conventional oven. □ *Vegetables* are at their best. Flavor and color are preserved and potatoes are fluffy. □ You'll want *scrambled eggs and bacon* for breakfast, lunch, and supper! Eggs are fluffier than in conventional cooking, and bacon cooks without turning or mess. □ *Cakes* are moist, rich and super-high. □ *Casseroles* cook without sticking and reheat with no trouble at all.

☐ *Candy and bar cookies* are particular favorites for microwave cooks because they are easy as pie. Try this Peanut Brittle or the zesty Lemon Bars and see for yourself. ☐ The microwave can't be beaten for *reheating leftover platters, rolls, and bread* so quickly they are truly perfect.

☐ Explore the pleasures of cooking *seafood* in your microwave oven. Fish fillets and steaks are moist and tender, their natural juices enhancing their delicate flavor. ☐ There's no equal to a *bowl of soup* or a cup of coffee served directly from the oven. ☐ *Melt butter (or chocolate)* in seconds and save the mess of burned pans or double boilers.

Now let's look at what you need to know to start cooking.

COOKING TECHNIQUES AND COOKWARE

In this chapter you will find everything you need to know to make microwave cooking easy, efficient, and pleasurable. Once you know the principles, the techniques will become second nature. Read this basic information with its accompanying illustrations carefully. Here you will learn why some foods cook faster than others, what you should know about timing and temperature, which cooking utensils and sizes are appropriate, and much more.

Because of the unique qualities of microwave energy, microwave cooking uses certain terms and methods that are different from those of conventional cooking. For example, in microwave cooking, many foods complete their cooking during standing time, either in the oven or after being removed from the oven. In addition, how food is arranged in the cooking dish is important to its being cooked evenly throughout.

ABOUT TIMING

Time is an important element in microwave cooking. But isn't that statement true for all cooking? You, the cook, have to be the judge, as you consider your family's preferences and use your own instincts. Be aware that even though the microwave oven is a superb product of computer technology, it is no more or less precise than any conventional cooking system. Nevertheless, because of the speed with which most food is cooked, timing is more crucial in microwave cooking than in conventional cooking. When you consider that a cooking task requiring one hour in a conventional oven generally needs only one-third, or less, of that time in a microwave oven, you can understand why, in microwave cooking, one minute can be the difference between overcooked or undercooked food. As a result, most microwave recipes express the probable minimum-maximum cooking times, as in "Use COOK cycle and cook 4 to 5 minutes." This direction is often assisted by a phrase such as "or until tender." As you become familiar with your oven you will recognize when to begin to check for doneness. Remember that it is better to undercook and add more cooking time than to overcook — then it's too late.

Cooking times might be precise if a way could be found to guarantee that all food would be exactly the same each time we cook it; if the utility company would guarantee not to alter our source of power (there are frequent changes in the voltage levels reaching our homes); and if the size, form, and content of food would be consistently the same. The fact is that one potato or one steak varies from another in density, moisture or fat content, shape, weight, and temperature. This is true of all food. The cook must be ready to adjust to the changes, to be flexible and observant. This discussion really comes down to the fact that you, not the microwave oven, are the cook. The oven can't make judgments, so you must. The recipes in this book have all been meticulously kitchen tested by expert home economists. You will find that the ranges of cooking times suggested are exact. As in all fine cooking, however, microwave cooking needs and benefits from a personal touch.

CHARACTERISTICS THAT AFFECT TIMING

Many characteristics of food, such as quantity, shape, density, and starting temperature affect timing. Understanding them will help you become a skilled and successful microwave cook.

Quantity

The larger the volume of food there is, the more time is needed to cook it. For example, one potato. may cook in 6 to 8 minutes but 2 potatoes take about one and a half times as long. If the quantity in a recipe is changed, be sure to make an adjustment in timing. When increasing a recipe, increase the amount of cooking time. Here is a general rule to follow: When doubling a recipe, increase the cooking time approximately 50 percent. When cutting a recipe in half, reduce the time by approximately 40 percent.

Density

Dense food such as potatoes, roast beef, and carrots takes longer to cook than porous food, such as cakes, ground beef, and apples, because it takes the microwaves longer to penetrate.

Irregularly-shaped food requires special arrangement (above). Moist food cooks faster than dry (above left). Food areas close to the oven top are shielded during cooking (left).

the denser texture. For example, a 2-pound roast will take longer than a 2-pound meat loaf.

Height

As in conventional cooking, areas that are closer to the energy source cook faster. In most microwave ovens, the energy source is at the top of the oven. Food close to the top may require shielding with pieces of aluminum foil or turning for even cooking.

Shape and Size

Thin food cooks faster than thick food; thin sections faster than thick. Small pieces also cook faster than large pieces. For even cooking, place thick pieces toward the outside of the dish, since the outside areas cook faster than the inside areas. For best results, try to cook pieces of similar size and shape together.

Moisture Content

Moist food cooks faster than dry food because microwave energy is easily absorbed by the moisture within the food. For example, 1 cup of sliced zucchini will cook faster than 1 cup of carrots because of the higher water content in the zucchini. In fact, the amount of free moisture within a food helps determine how rapidly it cooks.

Sugar and Fat Content

Food high in sugar and fat heats quicker than items low in these ingredients because microwave energy is attracted by sugar and fat. For example, the fruit or cheese filling of a sweet roll will heat faster than the roll itself and will be hotter, since sugar and fat reach higher temperatures than food low in sugar or fat content.

Delicate Ingredients

This term is used to refer to food that cooks so quickly in the microwave oven that it can overcook and toughen, separate, or curdle. For example, mayonnaise, cheese, eggs, cream, dairy sour cream, etc. Other food may "pop," such as snails, oysters, and chicken livers. For this reason, a lower power setting is often recommended for proper cooking. However, when these ingredients are mixed with other food, as in a casserole, stew, or soup, you may use a higher power setting, because volume automatically slows down the cooking.

Starting Temperature

As in conventional cooking, the temperature at which food is placed in the microwave oven affects the length of cooking time. More time is needed to cook food just out of the refrigerator than food at room temperature. For example, it takes longer to heat frozen green beans than canned green beans. Also, hot tap water will start boiling sooner than cold. Recipes in this book start with food at its normal storage temperature.

ABOUT UTENSILS

A wide variety of cookware and cooking implements can be used in the microwave oven. In order to indicate an item made of material that is safe and recommended for microwave cooking, we have created a new term, *microproof.* The Materials Checklist and Microproof Utensils Chart on the following pages will aid you in selecting the appropriate microproof utensil. Except for metal, most materials are microproof for at least a limited amount of cooking time. But unless specifically approved, items made of metal, even partially, are never to be used in the microwave oven, because they reflect microwaves, preventing them from passing through the cooking utensil into the food. In addition, metal that touches the oven sides will cause sparks, a static charge, known as arcing. Arcing is not harmful to you, though it will deface the oven. Metal twist ties or dishes or cups with gold or silver trim should not be used. See the Materials Checklist for those approved types of metal, such as pieces of aluminum foil, used as a shield over certain areas of food to prevent overcooking, or metal clips attached to frozen turkey.

When selecting a new piece of cookware, first check the manufacturer's directions. Also review the Materials Checklist and the Microproof Utensils Chart. If you are still in doubt, try this test: Pour a cup of water into a glass measure and place it in the oven next to the container or dish to be tested. Use COOK cycle and cook for 1 minute. If the new dish feels hot, don't use it — it is absorbing microwave energy. If it feels warm, the dish may only be used for warming food. If it remains at room temperature, it is *microproof.*

The rapid growth of microwave cooking has created many new products for use in the microwave oven. Among these are micro-proof replacements for cook-ware formerly available only in metal. You'll find a wide variety at your store — cake, bundt, and muffin pans, roasting racks, etc. When you add these to traditional microproof cookware and the array of microproof plastic and paper products, you'll find that microwave cooking enables you to select from many more kinds of cookware than available for con-ventional cooking.

Selecting Containers

Containers should accommodate the food being cooked. And you must make sure that they fit in your oven. For best results, try to use the particular size or shape of dish cited in a recipe. Varying the container size or shape may change cooking time.

Whenever possible use round or oval dishes. Square corners in cookware receive more micro-waves than the rest of the dish, so food in the corners tends to overcook. Some cake and loaf recipes call for ring molds or bundt pans to facilitate more even cooking. This is because the center area in a round or oval dish generally cooks more slowly than the outside. Round cook-ware with a small glass inserted open end up in the center also eliminates undercooked centers.

A 2-quart casserole called for in a recipe refers to a bowl-shaped cooking utensil. A 6×9-inch or a 9-inch round baking dish refers to a shallow cooking dish. In the case of puddings, sauces, and candies, fairly large containers are specified to pre-vent boiling over.

Materials Checklist

☐ CHINA, POTTERY: Ideal for microwave use. However, if they have metallic trim or glaze, they are not microproof and should not be used.

☐ GLASS: An excellent microwave cooking material. Especially useful for baking pies to check doneness of pie shells through the bottom. Since ovenproof glass is always safe, "microproof" is not mentioned in any recipe where a glass item is specified.

☐ METALS: *Not* suitable except as follows:

Small strips of aluminum foil can be used to cover areas on large pieces of meat or poultry that defrost or cook more rapidly than the rest of the piece — for example, a roast with jagged areas or thin ends, or the wing or breastbone of poultry. This method is known as *shielding* in microwave cooking.

Shallow aluminum TV dinner trays with foil covers removed can be heated, provided that the trays do not exceed 3/4 inch depth. However, this method only provides heating from the top, since the microwaves cannot penetrate the sides or bottom of the metal tray. It's best to "pop" the blocks of food out and place them on a dinner plate.

Frozen poultry containing metal clamps may be defrosted in the microwave oven without removing the clamps. Remove the clamps after defrosting.

Trays or any foil or metal item must be at least 1 inch from oven walls.

☐ PAPER: Approved for short-term cooking and for reheating. White paper towels, waxed paper, and parchment are suitable coverings. Extended use may cause the paper to burn. Must not be foil lined.

☐ PLASTICS: Excellent products have been designed for microwave use. Use plastics marked for microwave use and follow the directions of the manufacturer. Plastics that melt from the heat of the food should not be used.

☐ PLASTIC COOKING POUCHES: Can be used. Slit the pouch so steam can escape.

☐ STRAW AND WOOD: Can be used for quick warming. Be certain no metal is used on the straw or wood items.

Browning Dishes

A browning dish is used to sear, grill, fry, or brown food. It is made to absorb microwave energy. A special coating on the bottom of the dish becomes very hot when preheated in the microwave oven. For best results, follow the dish manufacturer's instructions.

After the dish is preheated, vegetable oil or butter may be added to enhance the browning and prevent food from sticking. After the food is placed on the preheated browning dish, the microwaves cook the interior of the food while the hot surface of the dish browns the exterior. The food is then turned over to brown the other side. The longer you wait to turn the food, the less browning occurs, since the dish cools off rapidly. You may need to drain the dish, wipe it, and preheat it again. Since the browning dish becomes very hot, be sure to use pot-holders.

Familiar items, such as muffin pans and molds, are available in microproof material. Other items, such as bacon racks and browning dishes, have been developed for microwave cooking (above). All kinds of paper products and many plastic ones make microwave cooking easy (above left). A wide variety of glass, ceramic, and wood products are perfect for microwave use (left).

A GUIDE TO MICROPROOF COOKWARE

ITEM	GOOD USE	GENERAL NOTES
China plates, cups	Heating dinners and drinks.	No metal trim.
Cooking pouches (plastic)	Cooking meat, vegetables, rice, other frozen food.	Slit pouch so steam can escape.
Corelle®	Heating dinners, soups, drinks.	Closed-handle cups should not be used.
Corning Ware® or Pyrex casseroles	Cooking main dishes, vegetables, desserts.	No metal trim.
Microwave browning dishes or grills	Searing, grilling, and frying small meat items; grilling sandwiches; frying eggs.	These utensils are specially made to absorb microwaves and preheat to high temperatures. They brown food that otherwise would not brown in a microwave oven.
Microwave roasting racks	Cooking roasts and chickens, squash and potatoes.	Special racks are available for cooking bacon.
Oven film and cooking bags	Cooking roasts or stews.	Substitute string for metal twist ties. Bag itself will not cause tenderizing. Do not use film with foil edges.
Paper plates, cups, napkins	Heating hot dogs, drinks, rolls, appetizers, sandwiches.	Absorbs moisture from baked goods and freshens them. Paper plates and cups with wax coatings should not be used.
Plastic wrap	Covering dishes.	Fold back edge to ventilate, allowing steam to escape.
Pottery and earthenware plates, mugs, etc.	Heating dinners, soups, drinks.	Some pottery has a metallic glaze. To check, use dish test (page 13).
Soft plastics, sherbet cartons	Reheating leftovers.	Used for very short reheating periods.
Thermometers	Measuring temperature of meat, poultry, and candy.	Use only approved microproof meat or candy thermometer in microwave oven.
TV dinner trays (aluminum)	Frozen dinners or homemade dinners.	No deeper than $\frac{3}{4}$ inch. Food will receive heat from top surface only. Foil covering food must be removed.
Waxed paper	Covering casseroles. Use as a tent.	Prevents splattering. Helps contain heat where a tight seal is not required. Food temperature may cause some melting.
Wooden spoons, wooden skewers, straw baskets	Stirring puddings and sauces; for shish kabobs, appetizers, warming breads.	Can withstand microwaves for short cooking periods. Be sure no metal fittings on wood or straw.

ABOUT METHODS

The evenness and speed of microwave cooking are affected not only by the characteristics of food but also by certain cooking methods. Some of these techniques are used in conventional cooking as well, but they are particularly important with microwave cooking. Many other important variables are included here.

Microwave arrangement methods create unique cook-and-serve opportunities, such as the vegetable platter above. Chicken legs look like the spokes in a wheel

Arrangement

The way food is arranged in the dish and in the oven enhances even cooking and speeds defrosting and cooking food. Microwaves penetrate the outer portion of food first; therefore, food should be arranged so that the denser, thicker areas are near the dish edge, and the thinner, more porous areas are near the center. For example, when cooking broccoli, split the heavy stalks to expose more area, then overlap florets. Chicken legs are arranged like the spokes of a wheel, with the bony end toward the center. This gives even density to the food and provides even cooking. Place shrimp in a ring with the tails toward the center. Food such as cupcakes or potatoes should be arranged in a circle, not in rows.

Turning Over

As in conventional cooking, some food, such as large roasts, whole poultry, a ham, or hamburgers, may require turning over to brown each side and to promote even heating. Any food seared on the browning dish should be turned over. During the defrosting process in the microwave oven, it is often necessary to turn food.

Rotating

Some food, such as pies and cakes, that cannot be stirred, turned over, or rearranged, calls for repositioning the cooking dish one-quarter turn to allow for even distribution of the microwave energy. Rotate only if the baked food is not cooking or rising evenly. Most food does not need to be rotated.

Turning (above), rotating (above left), and stirring (left) assist in even cooking.

Stirring

Less stirring is required in micro-wave cooking than in conventional cooking. When necessary, stir from the outside to the center, since the outside heats faster than the center portion. Stirring blends the flavors and promotes even heating. Stir only as directed in the recipes. Constant stirring is never required in microwave cooking.

Rearranging

Sometimes food that cannot be stirred needs repositioning in the cooking utensil to allow even heating. When rearranging food, move the center food to the outside of the dish and the outer food toward the center.

Piercing

It is essential to pierce the skin or membrane of certain food, such as egg yolks, potatoes, liver, eggplant, and squash. Because they retain moisture during cooking, they must be pierced to prevent bursting and to allow steam to escape. A toothpick may be used for egg yolks; a fork is best for potatoes and squash.

Types of covers for microwave cooking (above). Piercing is important with certain food (above right). The effect of standing time on a roast (right).

Covering

Covers are used to trap steam, prevent dehydration, speed cooking, and help food retain its natural moisture. Suitable tight coverings are microproof casserole tops, glass covers, plastic wraps, oven bags, and microproof plates and saucers. Remove coverings away from your face to prevent steam burns. Paper toweling is especially useful as a light covering to prevent splatter and to absorb moisture. Waxed paper helps retain heat and moisture.

Standing Time

This term refers to the time food needs to complete cooking or thawing after the microwave time has ended. During standing time, heat continues to be conducted from the outside to the center of the food. After the oven is turned off, food may remain in the oven for standing time or may be placed on a heatproof counter. This procedure is an essential part of food preparation with the microwave oven. Some food, such as roasts, requires standing time to attain the proper internal temperature for rare, medium, or well-done. Casseroles need standing time to allow the heat to spread evenly and to complete reheating or cooking. With cakes, pies, and quiches, standing time permits the center to finish cooking. During the standing time outside the oven, place food on a flat surface, such as a heat-resistant breadboard or counter top, not on a cooling rack as you would conventionally.

Shielding

Certain thin or bony areas, such as the wing tips of poultry, the head and tail of fish, or the breastbone of a turkey, cook faster than thicker areas. Covering these parts with small pieces of aluminum foil shields these areas from overcooking, since aluminum foil reflects the waves. Be careful not to allow the foil to touch the oven walls.

Browning

Some food does not brown in the microwave oven as much as in the conventional oven. Depending upon the fat content, most food will brown in 8 to 10 minutes in the microwave oven. For example, bacon browns in minutes because of its high fat content. For food that cooks too quickly to brown, such as ham-burgers, fried eggs, steak or cutlets, a special browning dish is available. A longer cooking time, or higher fat content will provide more browning. You can also create a browned look by brushing on a browning agent, such as gravy mix, onion soup mix, etc. Cakes, bread, and pie shells do not brown. Using chocolate, spices, or dark flour helps attain the dark color. Or you can create appealing color by adding frostings or dark spices.

High Altitude Adjustments

As in conventional cooking, microwave cooking at high altitudes requires adjustments in cooking time for leavened products like bread and cake. Other foods may require a slightly longer cooking time to become tender, since water boils at a lower temperature. Usually, for every 3 minutes of microwave cooking time you add 1 minute for the higher altitude. Therefore, a recipe calling for 3 minutes needs 4 minutes and a recipe requiring 6 minutes needs 8 minutes. The wisest procedure is to start with the time given in the recipe and then check for doneness. Adding time is easy, but overcooking can be a real problem.

GETTING TO KNOW YOUR OVEN

Your new Sanyo microwave oven gives you the simplicity of easy-to-use controls combined with the marvel of space-age speed in cooking. An easily-understood control panel will soon be as familiar to you as the controls on your conventional range.

The oven has a TIMER that enables you to set recipe times given in the recipes and in the Cooking Guides throughout this book. The TIMER also controls the start of the cooking process on some models, while others have a separate START button. In either case, the oven stops automatically when the door is opened or when the time set with the TIMER has elapsed.

Some oven models offer two cooking cycles or power levels and have push buttons designated COOK and DEFROST. Ovens with a single-power cook cycle simply control cooking with the TIMER and START button, or with the TIMER alone. Recipes in this book specify either COOK or DEFROST cycles. Consult your Use and Care Manual if your oven does not have a separate defrost button. Please keep in mind, too, that the Use and Care Manual is the best source for information about your particular oven model.

Can We Help?

Sometimes, discovering the joys of a new appliance can be frustrating, can't it? I thought we'd take a moment at this point to let you know that we want you to become as comfortable and expert with your new oven as you are with your other kitchen appliances.

The "Cooking School" this book presents, coupled with your Use and Care Manual, may be all the help you need. But if you do have any questions that are not answered here or need additional assistance, please write me:

Thelma Pressman
Director, Consumer Education
*   & Services*
SANYO ELECTRIC, INC.
200 Riser Road
Little Ferry, New Jersey 07643

Internal Temperature

As in conventional cooking, the most accurate way to gauge doneness is with a food thermometer. However, you *cannot use a conventional meat thermometer* with the microwave oven because it may cause sparks, a static charge, known as arcing. Arcing is not harmful to you, though it will deface the oven. Specially designed food thermometers are available for microwave use and some can also be used in your conventional oven. Carefully check the thermometer manufacturer's instructions.

The "Guide to Internal Temperatures" provides a range from 120°F to 180°F. Keep in mind that standing time is essential for most food to reach its optimum serving temperature and quality. So, the temperatures in the Guide are 5 to 15 degrees *below* the desired ready-to-carve or eat internal temperature. Be-

Specially designed microwave food thermometers are a valuable aid to accurate determination of doneness.

cause of the nature of microwave energy, during standing time the temperature of most food rises about 5° to 15°F. For example, after 10 minutes of standing time, the temperature of rare beef will reach 135°F; well done lamb will reach its proper 170° to 180°F.

Guide to Internal Temperatures*

Suggested Thermometer Readings	
120°	Rare Beef, Fully Cooked Ham
130°	Medium Beef
140°	Fish Steaks and Fillets, Well Done Beef
150°	Vegetables, Hot Drinks, Soups, Casseroles
155°	Veal
165°	Well Done Lamb, Pork
170°	Poultry Parts, Whole Fish
180°	Well Done Whole Poultry

*Refer to individual Cooking Guides (see Index) for specific instructions.

Microwave Thermometer Use

As in conventional cooking, the thermometer must be carefully and properly inserted in the food to obtain the best results. Do not allow the thermometer — and, again, remember we are talking about a *special microwave thermometer* — to touch bone or fat.

False readings may result. Here are a few tips.

☐ For *roasts*, place the thermometer in the roast about equal distance between the ends. The tip should be inserted until it reaches the approximate center of the meat.

☐ For *poultry*, place the thermometer between the body and the inner thigh. Avoid bone.

☐ Check *defrosting* food with the thermometer. If the dial drops to a lower temperature or the thermometer cannot be inserted, you know that the food has not reached room temperature or is still frozen.

☐ In *reheating* food, a microwave thermometer can be valuable to obtain exact temperatures for casseroles, soups, and leftovers. (150°F to 170°F are good temperature guides for soups, casseroles, etc.)

☐ In *candy making*, temperature checks are especially helpful. You can obtain microproof candy thermometers but keep in mind that space in the oven is limited. You can check candy mixture temperatures *outside the oven* with a conventional candy thermometer.

Reheating

One of the major assets of the microwave oven is its efficiency in reheating cooked food. Not only does most food reheat quickly, but it also retains moisture and its just-cooked flavor when properly arranged and covered. If someone is late for dinner, there's no need to fret. Just place a microproof plate containing the cooked food in your oven; in moments, dinner is ready once again. Reheat food in serving dishes or on paper plates and save extra cleanup time. Take-out food, which usually arrives at your home cooled off, can be easily reheated in seconds to its original state in your microwave oven. No more cold pizzas or lukewarm hamburgers. Leftovers are a treat, too. You may even want to prepare food the day before, refrigerate, and serve the following day. You'll no longer call food leftovers, because it will taste as if "just made." Follow the tips below to help get excellent results when you are reheating food.

☐ To arrange a combination of different foods on a plate, place the dense food, like meat, at the outer edges and the more porous food, like breads, toward the center. Food that cooks most quickly should be placed at the center, with slower cooking food at the edges.

☐ Dense food, such as mashed potatoes and casseroles, cooks more quickly and evenly if a depression is made in the center, or if the food is shaped in a ring.

☐ To retain moisture during reheating, cover food with plastic wrap or a microproof lid. Wrap breads and sandwiches in paper toweling to absorb moisture and prevent sogginess. Use waxed paper to hold heat in and still allow steam to escape.

☐ Spread food out in a shallow container rather than piling it high, for quicker and more even heating.

☐ As a general guide to reheating a plate of food, start with $1\frac{1}{2}$ to 2 minutes, then check for doneness. If the plate on which the food is cooked feels warm, the food is probably heated through, for its warmth has heated the plate. Because of the numerous variables in the food to be reheated, i.e., amount, shape, food characteristics, starting temperature, etc., recommended heating times can only be approximate.

Defrosting

One of the great attractions of the microwave oven is its ability to defrost raw food or heat frozen cooked food. You need only to choose the DEFROST cycle, or follow the Use and Care Manual's instructions, to observe the swiftness and ease of defrosting.

Many of the same principles and techniques that apply to microwave cooking also apply to microwave defrosting. Microwaves are attracted to water or moisture molecules. As soon as microwaves have defrosted a portion of the item, they are more attracted to the thawed portion. The frozen portion continues to thaw, but this is due to the heat in the thawed portion. Special techniques, such as shielding and rotating, are helpful to be sure the thawed portion does not cook before the rest defrosts. It is often necessary to turn, stir, and separate to assist the defrosting process. Defrosting requires standing time to complete. Because food differs in size, weight, and density, recommended defrosting times can only be approximate. Additional standing time may be necessary to defrost com-

Many foods can begin defrosting in their original wrappers (above). Remove thawed portions of ground beef so that cooking does not start. Fish fillets and thin meat slices should be separated as soon as possible (right).

pletely. Read the Defrosting Guides throughout the book for times and special instructions about defrosting specific foods. Here are some tips to aid you toward fast and easy defrosting.

☐ Poultry, seafood, fish, and meat may begin defrosting in their original closed package. Remove as soon as possible and place on dish to provide more even thawing and to prevent partial cooking from steam that could be produced in the sealed package. You may leave metal clips in poultry during defrosting, but you should remove them as soon as possible before cooking. Replace metal twists on bags with string or rubber bands before defrosting.

☐ Plastic-wrapped packages from the supermarket meat department may not be wrapped with a plastic wrap recommended for microwave use. If in doubt, unwrap package and place food on a microproof plate.

☐ Vegetables are usually packaged to go right into the microwave for defrosting and heating to serving temperature. It is not necessary to use a DEFROST setting for frozen vegetables. They are prepared on the COOK setting.

☐ Poultry wings, legs, and the small or bony ends of meat or fish may need to be covered with pieces of aluminum foil for part of the thawing time to prevent cooking while the remainder thaws.

☐ Large items should be turned and rotated halfway through defrosting time to provide more even thawing.

☐ Food textures influence thawing time. Because of air space, porous food like bread defrosts more quickly than a solid mass, such as a roast.

☐ The edges will begin cooking if meat, fish, and seafood are completely thawed in the microwave oven. Therefore, food should still be icy in the center when removed from oven. It will finish thawing while standing.

☐ To thaw half of a frozen vegetable package, wrap half the package with aluminum foil. When unwrapped side is thawed, separate and return balance to freezer.

☐ Thin or sliced items, such as fish fillets, meat patties, etc., should be separated as soon as possible. Remove thawed pieces and allow others to continue thawing.

☐ Casseroles, saucy foods, vegetables, and soups should be stirred once or twice during defrosting to redistribute heat.

☐ Frozen fried foods may be defrosted but will not be crisp when heated in the microwave oven.

☐ Freezing tips: It is helpful to freeze in small quantities rather than in one large piece. When freezing casseroles, it's a good idea to insert an empty paper cup in the center so no food is present there. This speeds thawing. Depressing the center of ground meat before freezing also hastens thawing later. Take care to wrap and package food well.

LET'S USE THE OVEN

Now it's time for some practical experience using all the features of the microwave oven: first, a quick hot drink, then, a scrambled egg. Let's begin.

Lesson One
A quick pick-me-up

Take your favorite mug or cup; be sure there is no gold or silver trim or metallic glaze. If you are not certain that your mug is microproof, test it as directed on page 13. Then follow these step-by-step directions:

1. Fill mug or cup with water and place in the center of the oven. Close the oven door.

2. Push the COOK button to select the COOK cycle. *(Oven models without a COOK button eliminate this step.)*

3. Turn the TIMER to 2 minutes. *(Oven models without a START button will begin cooking. Eliminate step 4.)*
4. Now push the START button.
5. The timer will beep when 2 minutes are up. The oven turns off automatically. Open the door.
6. Remove the mug. The handle will be cool enough to hold and the cup itself will be warm from the heated water.
7. Stir in instant coffee, tea, or instant soup.

Lesson Two
Scrambled Egg

1. Break egg into a microproof bowl or 2-cup glass measure. Add 1 tablespoon milk. Beat with a fork. Add 1 teaspoon butter or margarine.
2. Cover with waxed paper. Place in oven and close door.

3. Push the COOK button to select the COOK cycle. *(Oven models without a COOK button eliminate this step.)*

4. Turn the TIMER to 1½ minutes. *(Oven models without a START button will begin cooking. Eliminate step 5.)*

5. Now push START button.
6. When 40-45 seconds have passed, open oven door. Oven will stop. Stir egg mixture briskly. Return to oven; close door. *(Oven models without START button continue to cook. Eliminate step 7.)*

7. Push START button to complete cooking sequence.
8. When TIMER beeps, egg is done.
9. Let egg stand 1 minute before serving — just time to toast some bread. Now enjoy breakfast. (Whatever the time of day, this will be the best scrambled egg you've ever tasted!)

ON YOUR OWN

You will undoubtedly want to cook some of your favorite conventional recipes in the microwave oven. With a little thought and experimenting, you can convert many recipes. Before converting a recipe, study it to determine if it will adapt well to microwave cooking. Look for a recipe in this book that matches your own recipe most closely. For example, find a recipe with the same amount, type, and form of main ingredient, such as 1 pound ground meat or 2 pounds beef cut in 1-inch pieces, etc. Then compare other ingredients, such as pasta or vegetables. The microwave recipe will probably call for less liquid, because there is so little evaporation in microwave cooking. At the beginning of each recipe chapter hints on adapting recipes are provided. Also use the following guidelines:

- ☐ Candies, bar cookies, meatloaf, and certain baked goods may not need adjustments in ingredients. For some cakes, sauces, gravies, and certain casseroles, liquids should be reduced or thickening agents increased.

- ☐ Many casseroles will require adjustment in the order in which ingredients are added. Certain ingredients, such as long-grain rice, take longer to cook than others. When converting to microwave, substitute a quicker-cooking ingredient, such as precooked rice.

For example, substitute instant onion flakes for chopped onion, and cut vegetable ingredients, such as carrots, in smaller pieces than the conventional recipe recommends.

☐ Most converted recipes will require adjustments in cooking time. Although a "rule of thumb" always has exceptions, you can generally assume that most microwave recipes are heated in about one-quarter to one-third of the conventional recipe time. Check for doneness after one-quarter of the time before continuing to cook.

Cooking Casseroles

The microwave oven is exceptionally good for cooking casseroles. Vegetables keep their bright fresh color and crisp texture. Meat is tender and flavorful. Here are some general hints to help you:

☐ Most casseroles can be made ahead of time, refrigerated or frozen, then reheated later in the microwave.

☐ Casseroles are usually covered with plastic wrap or glass lids during cooking.

☐ Allow casseroles to stand 5 to 10 minutes before serving, according to size. Standing time completes cooking of the casserole center.

☐ You will obtain best results if you make ingredients uniform in size, stirring occasionally to distribute heat. If the ingredients are of different sizes, stir more often.

☐ Casseroles containing less tender meat need longer simmering. Those work well on the DEFROST cycle which gives a slow-cooker effect. Casseroles with delicate ingredients such as cream or cheese sauces often profit from the DEFROST cycle, too. Cheese toppings should be added for the last 1 or 2 minutes.

☐ When used in quick-cooking casseroles, celery, onions, green peppers, and carrots should be sautéed before being added to dish. Rice or noodles should be partially cooked before combining with cooked meat, fish, or poultry.

About Lower Calories

Scattered throughout the book are low-calorie suggestions and low-calorie recipes. They are listed in the index so you can find them when you need them. In general, you can lower calories in many recipes by making substitutions such as these:

☐ Bouillon or water for butter when sautéing or softening vegetables.

☐ Vegetables for potatoes or pasta.

☐ Lean meats for fatty ones.

☐ Skim milk for whole milk.

☐ Skim milk cheeses like low-fat cottage, ricotta, and mozzarella for creamy fatty ones.

☐ Natural gravy with herbs for cream and butter sauces.

☐ Fruit cooked in its natural juices for fruit with sugar added.

☐ Skinless chicken breast for regular cut-up chicken.

☐ Shellfish, and white fish such as sole, halibut, and flounder for mackerel, tuna, and other oily fish.

By the Way . . .

To get the greatest pleasure out of your microwave oven, keep in mind that certain food is best done by conventional means of cooking. For the following reasons, we don't recommend:

☐ Eggs cooked in the shell, because the light membrane surrounding the yolk collects energy, which then causes a steam build-up that will explode the egg. Don't experiment. It's a mess to clean up!

☐ Deep-fat frying, because the confined environment of the oven is not suited to the handling of the food or oil and is not safe.

☐ Pancakes, because no crust forms. (But the oven is great for reheating pancakes, waffles, and similar items.)

☐ Toasting, because it also requires crust development.

☐ Popovers, because of the slow steam development necessary to make them rise.

☐ Home canning, because it is impossible to judge exact boiling temperatures inside the jars and you cannot be sure that the temperature and cooking time are sufficient to prevent contamination of the food.

☐ Chiffon and angel food cakes, because they require steady, dry heat to rise and be tender.

☐ Heating bottles with small necks, like those for syrups and toppings, because they are apt to break from the pressure build-up.

☐ Large items, such as a 25-pound turkey or a dozen baking potatoes, because the space is not adequate and no time is saved.

☐ True soufflés, because. the microwaves tend to make dishes high in egg content a bit rubbery.

About popcorn:

Do not attempt to pop corn in a paper bag, since the corn may dehydrate and overheat, causing the paper bag to catch on fire. Due to the many variables, such as the age of the corn and its moisture content, popping corn in the microwave oven is not recommended. Microwave popping devices are available. While safe to use, they usually do not give results equal to those of conventional popping methods. If the microwave device is used, carefully follow the instructions provided with the product.

School's Out!

Well, not quite. Throughout the recipe chapters, you'll find helpful information to add to your microwave cooking knowledge. A hint: reread these first 32 pages when you have a spare moment. And, trust us! You'll soon be "best on the block" as a microwave cook.

Now, go ahead, enjoy your oven!

STARTERS AND SNACKS

Tangy Beef Balls (page 39) and Nacho Rounds (page 42) are arranged in the circular microwave pattern (left). Arrange drinks the same way (above).

Whether you choose to call them tidbits, snacks, or appetizers, they always rate high with the family and guests. The incredible speed of the microwave oven makes all the last-minute hustle and hassle disappear. You can really be part of the party!

Start off a special family meal with Tomato Jalapeño Cheese Dip (page 40) or Olive and Bacon Wraps (page 42). If you want to surprise friends during the next "come-on-over" night, Chicken Wings Canton (page 40) and Party Franks (page 38) will surely make them wonder where you found the time to fuss.

Hot drinks are in this chapter, too, because they sure can make any snack a special treat.

And how about those days when the kids drag in from school, so down in the dumps that you don't know what to do? Perk up their day with Muffin Toppers (page 36) and a friendly mug of our Country Cocoa (page 36).

Converting Your Recipes

Most of your favorite hot appetizers will adapt well to microwave cooking, except those wrapped in pastry. Pastry requires the hot environment of the conventional oven to become crisp. The recipe for Olive and Bacon Wraps (page 42) is an ideal guide for countless appetizers containing seafood, chicken, vegetable, and fruit combinations. Here are some tips:

☐ Toppings for canapés can be made ahead but do not place on bread or crackers until just before heating. This assures a crisp base.

☐ Cover appetizers or dips only when the recipe specifies doing so. Use fitted glass lids, waxed paper, plastic wrap, or paper towels.

☐ Compare your favorite dip recipe with one of the choices here to determine your microwave time.

☐ While the microwave oven is not recommended for baking pastry appetizers, it is perfect for reheating such items.

COOKING GUIDE — CONVENIENCE APPETIZERS

Food	Amount	Control	Time	Special Notes
Canned meat spread	4 oz.	COOK	45 - 60 seconds	Transfer to small microproof bowl.
Canned sausages, cocktail sausages	5 oz.	COOK	2 - 2½ minutes	Place in covered glass casserole.
Cocktail franks, pizza roll	4 servings	COOK	1 - 1½ minutes	Place on paper towels. Roll will not crisp.
Cooked pizza, 10 inches, cut in 8 portions	1 wedge	COOK	1 - 1½ minutes	Place on paper towels or paper plate or leave in uncovered cardboard box, points toward center.
	4 wedges	COOK	2 - 2½ minutes	
	Whole	COOK	3½ - 4½ minutes	
Dips, cream	½ cup	DEFROST	30 - 50 seconds	Cover with plastic wrap.
Eggrolls, pastry-covered	2 servings	COOK	40 - 60 seconds	Place on paper towels, do not cover.

COOKING GUIDE — HOT DRINKS
Use COOK cycle.

Liquid	6-ounce Cup	Time (minutes)	8-ounce Cup	Time (minutes)	Special Notes
Water	1	1½-1¾	1	2-2½	For instant
	2	2-2½	2	3½-4	coffee, tea, etc.
Milk	1	2½-3	1	3-3½	For cocoa, etc.
	2	3-3½	2	3½-4	
Reheating	1	1½-1¾	1	1½-2	
coffee	2	2¼-2¾	2	2½-3¼	

Deviled Ham Triangles —————— 14 servings
Total Cooking Time: 4 to 5 minutes

7 slices white or whole
   wheat bread
1 can (4½ ounces)
   deviled ham
2 teaspoons Burgundy
Dash freshly ground
   pepper
1 egg white
3 tablespoons mayonnaise
1 teaspoon dry mustard
Paprika

Trim crusts from bread; toast. Cut toast diagonally into triangles. In small bowl, combine ham, burgundy, and pepper; blend well. Spread on toast triangles. In small mixing bowl, beat egg white until stiff; fold in mayonnaise and mustard. Spread over ham mixture. Place triangles in circle on paper towel-lined microproof plate. Use COOK cycle and cook 4 to 5 minutes, or until egg white is set, rotating plate every 2 minutes. Sprinkle each serving with dash of paprika. Let stand 2 minutes before serving.

Beef Muffin Toppers —————— 2 servings
Total Cooking Time: 2 minutes

⅓ cup lean ground beef
1 English muffin, split and
   toasted
1 teaspoon salt
½ teaspoon garlic powder
Dash freshly ground
   pepper
¼ cup shredded Cheddar or
   1 slice processed
   Cheddar cheese, halved

Divide beef and spread with a knife on muffin halves. Sprinkle garlic powder, salt, and pepper evenly on muffin halves. Place on microproof plate. Use COOK cycle and cook 2 minutes. Sprinkle shredded cheese or place ½ slice cheese on each serving. Let stand 1 minute, or until cheese is melted. Serve hot.

Country Cocoa ———————————— 1 serving
Total Cooking Time: 3 to 3½ minutes

1 cup milk
1 tablespoon sugar
1 tablespoon unsweetened
 cocoa powder
1 drop vanilla
1 large marshmallow (optional)

In 2-cup glass measure, combine milk, sugar, cocoa, and vanilla. Use COOK cycle and cook 3 to 3½ minutes, stirring after 1 minute. Pour into mug and top with marshmallow.

To reduce calories, substitute 1 cup skim milk for milk. Add artificial sweetener equal to sugar, or to taste. Use cinnamon stick as stirrer, if desired.

Muffin Toppers ———————————— 2 servings
Total Cooking Time: 2 minutes

1 tablespoon butter or
 margarine
½ teaspoon prepared mustard
1 English muffin, split and
 toasted
½ cup chopped or 2 slices
 cooked ham
½ cup shredded cheese
 (Swiss, mozzarella,
 Cheddar, or Monterey
 Jack)

Thoroughly blend butter and mustard; spread on muffin halves. Divide ham between muffins. Top with cheese. Place on microproof plate. Use DEFROST cycle and cook 2 minutes. Let stand 1 minute before serving.

Leftover cooked meat or poultry can also be used for toppers. Thinly slice or cube and pile on muffins. Try adding sauerkraut, pickles, or toppings of your choice.

For 4 servings, place muffins in a circle on microproof plate. Use DEFROST cycle and cook 4 minutes.

Chili Bean Dip ———————————— 2 cups
Total Cooking Time: 6 to 7 minutes

1 can (15 ounces) chili
   with beans
8 ounces process American
   cheese, diced
2 drops hot pepper sauce

Place chili in container of blender. Cover and process until smooth. Pour into 1½-quart microproof bowl. Add cheese and hot pepper sauce. Use DEFROST cycle and cook 6 minutes, or until cheese is melted, stirring once during cooking time. Blend well. Serve with corn or tortilla chips.

Party Franks ———————————— 10 to 12 servings
Total Cooking Time: 11 minutes

1½ pounds frankfurters
1 jar (10 ounces) cranberry
   jelly
2 tablespoons prepared
   mustard

Cut each frankfurter crosswise into 4 sections. Cut each section in half lengthwise to make 8 pieces. Split ends of each piece within ¼-inch of the center; set aside. Combine jelly and mustard in 2-quart microproof casserole. Use DEFROST cycle and cook 6 minutes, or until jelly is melted, stirring after 3 minutes. Add frankfurters; stir to coat. Cover with waxed paper. Use COOK cycle and cook 5 minutes, or until hot. Stir and let stand, covered, 3 minutes. Serve with cocktail picks.

Spiced Cider ———————————— 1 quart
Total Cooking Time: 20 minutes

1 quart apple cider
¼ cup firmly packed light
   brown sugar
½ teaspoon whole cloves
½ teaspoon whole allspice
1 cinnamon stick
   Dash salt

Combine all ingredients in 2-quart microproof casserole. Use DEFROST cycle and cook 20 minutes, or until hot. Remove spices. Serve hot, garnished with slices of red apple, if desired.

Tangy Beef Balls ———————————— 4 dozen
Total Cooking Time: 12 to 16 minutes

½ cup butter-flavored
   cracker crumbs
⅓ cup evaporated milk
¼ cup salt
1 tablespoon instant minced
   onion
2 teaspoons curry powder
1 pound lean ground beef

Combine crumbs, milk, salt, onion, and curry; mix lightly. Add beef and blend thoroughly. Shape mixture into 48 1-inch balls. Arrange half of the balls in a double circle on a round microproof plate. Cover with waxed paper. Use COOK cycle and cook 6 to 8 minutes, or until beef is no longer red, rotating dish once during cooking time. Repeat with remaining meatballs. Serve on toothpicks.

If sauce is desired, melt 1 package (10 ounces) frozen Welsh Rabbit in 1-quart microproof casserole. Use COOK cycle and cook 5 to 6 minutes, or until hot, stirring as soon as melted and again during cooking time. Pour over meatballs, stirring to coat.

Roasted Soybean Nuts ———————— 3½ cups
Total Cooking Time: 55 to 70 minutes

2 cups dried soybeans
5 cups water
¼ cup vegetable oil
   Salt

Soak soybeans in water to cover overnight. Add additional water, if necessary. Drain. In 4-quart glass bowl, cover soybeans with 5 cups water. Use COOK cycle and cook 30 to 40 minutes, or until soft; skim and stir every 5 minutes. Drain; spread on paper towels until dry. In 10-inch glass pie plate, mix 2 cups of the cooked soft beans with 2 tablespoons of the oil; stir to coat. Use COOK cycle and cook 25 to 30 minutes, or until crisp, stirring frequently, especially after 20 minutes. Spread on paper towels; sprinkle lightly with salt. Repeat with remaining beans and oil. Store in airtight container.

Chicken Wings Canton ———— 2 to 4 servings
Total Cooking Time: 18 to 20 minutes

6 chicken wings
¼ cup soy sauce
½ cup fine cracker crumbs
½ teaspoon garlic powder
½ teaspoon paprika
¼ teaspoon ginger
⅛ teaspoon freshly ground
 pepper

Cut wings in half; discard tips, or save for use in chicken broth. Rinse; pat dry with paper towels. Pour soy sauce into shallow bowl; set aside. In another shallow bowl, combine remaining ingredients. Dip chicken in soy sauce; roll in seasoned crumbs, coating evenly. Arrange chicken wings, skin-side up in spoke pattern in 9-inch round glass pie plate, placing thickest portions toward outside of plate. Cover with paper towels. Use COOK cycle and cook 10 minutes. Rotate dish one-quarter turn. Use COOK cycle and cook 8 to 10 minutes, or until chicken is tender. Serve hot.

Tomato Jalapeño Cheese Dip —— about 4 cups
Total Cooking Time: 7 minutes

2 pounds process American
 cheese, cubed
1 can (1½ ounces) tomatoes
 and jalapeño peppers,
 drained
1 can (5.3 ounces)
 evaporated milk

Combine all ingredients in 2-quart glass measure or microproof bowl. Use COOK cycle and cook 7 minutes, or until cheese is melted, stirring once during cooking time. Blend thoroughly with electric mixer. Pour into serving bowl. Serve with corn chips or dipping-style potato chips.

Extra dip can be frozen in plastic containers. To reheat, use DEFROST cycle and cook 1 minute. Stir and repeat until dipping consistency.

Olive and Bacon Wraps —————— 2 dozen

Total Cooking Time: 26 minutes

12 slices bacon
1 jar (4¾ ounces) large
 stuffed green olives,
 (about 24), drained
2 tablespoons brown sugar,
 divided

Cut bacon slices in half. Wrap a piece of bacon around each olive, securing with a toothpick. Place half of the olives in a circle on a paper towel-lined microproof plate. Sprinkle with 1 tablespoon of sugar. Cover with a paper towel. Use COOK cycle and cook 10 minutes. Turn olives over. Cover. Use COOK cycle and cook 3 minutes, or until bacon is cooked. Let stand 1 minute before serving. Repeat with remaining olives.

Nacho Rounds —————————— 4 to 6 servings

Total Cooking Time: 8 to 10 minutes

1 package (8 ounces)
 tortilla chips
2 cups shredded Cheddar
 cheese
1 can (4 ounces) diced
 green chilies, drained
1 can (2¼ ounces) chopped
 black olives, drained

Arrange chips on 2 10-inch microproof serving platters. Cover each with cheese, chilies, and olives. Use DEFROST cycle and cook, 1 plate at a time, 4 to 5 minutes, or until cheese is melted.

Shrimp Cream Cheese Dip ———————— 2 cups
Total Cooking Time: 3 to 4 minutes

1 package (8 ounces) cream
   cheese, quartered
1 can (7 ounces) broken
   shrimp, drained
2 tablespoons catsup or
   chili sauce
1 teaspoon instant minced
   onion
1 teaspoon prepared mustard
1 teaspoon Worcestershire
   sauce
¼ teaspoon garlic powder

Combine all ingredients in 1-quart microproof casserole. Use COOK cycle and cook 3 to 4 minutes, or until warm, stirring once during cooking time. Stir; serve with crackers or chips.

To reduce calories, substitute low-fat Neufchatel for cream cheese and substitute raw vegetables for crackers or chips. Zucchini rounds are especially nice and can even be topped with the dip, as a spread.

Wine Warmer ————————————— 8 servings
Total Cooking Time: 10 minutes

⅕ gallon full-bodied red
   wine
3 teaspoons sugar
   Orange peel, cut in
   2-inch strips
2 cinnamon sticks

Combine all ingredients in 2-quart glass measure or microproof bowl. Use DEFROST cycle and cook 10 minutes. Do not boil. Serve in mugs garnished with an orange slice.

Liver Brandy Spread ——————— 3 cups
Total Cooking Time: 9 minutes

1 pound chicken livers,
   rinsed and drained
1 small onion, chopped
½ cup diced celery
¼ cup unsalted butter
1 clove garlic, halved
   Dash freshly ground
   pepper
2 tablespoons brandy
1 hard-cooked egg, chopped

Pierce livers in several places with toothpick. Combine livers, onion, celery, butter, garlic, and pepper in 2-quart microproof casserole. Cover. Use COOK cycle and cook 6 minutes, stirring once during cooking time. Use COOK cycle and cook, uncovered, 3 minutes, or until livers are no longer pink. Let stand, covered, 10 minutes. Purée liver mixture and brandy in container of electric blender or food processor. Pour into serving bowl. Sprinkle with egg. Chill thoroughly 3 to 4 hours, before serving.

Hot Crab and Sherry Dip —————— 2 cups
Total Cooking Time: 4 minutes

1 package (8 ounces) cream
  cheese, quartered
2 tablespoons sherry
2 tablespoons milk
1 tablespoon instant minced
  onion
1½ teaspoons grated lemon
  rind
1 teaspoon horseradish
⅛ teaspoon garlic powder
1 can (7 ounces) crab meat,
  drained and flaked

Place cheese in 1-quart microproof casserole. Use COOK cycle and cook 1 minute, or until softened. Stir in remaining ingredients, except crab, until smooth. Stir in crab. Spread evenly in casserole. Use COOK cycle and cook 3 minutes, or until warm. Stir. Sprinkle with paprika before serving, if desired. Serve with crackers, toast rounds, or crisp vegetables.

SOUPER DUPER SANDWICHES

A microproof plate makes a dandy cover for a microproof bowl when preparing soup (right). Microwave browning dishes can enhance the flavor and appearance of hamburgers (above).

Yes, indeed, soup is super when prepared in the microwave oven! You can prepare canned or instant soup right in the serving bowl or mug. But don't you agree that nothing is more reassuring than a steaming bowl of your very own homemade soup? Now, you'll prepare your own more often. Imagine the convenience of cooking in the serving tureen (any nice and large casserole will do) and then ladling leftover soup from the refrigerator container into a mug for reheating and serving. No pan to clean!

Sandwiches, too, are so easy and most can be prepared simply wrapped in waxed paper or paper towels.

Best of all, of course, are the marvelous soup and sandwich combinations you can serve for lunch, brunch, or a quick dinner. Here are two of our selections: Manhattan Seafood Chowder (page 52) with Tuna, Tomato and Cheese (page 60). Quick Minestrone (page 51) with Ranch Burgers (page 59).

Converting Your Recipes

An enormous variety of sandwich combinations can be made in your microwave oven. Sandwiches heat quickly, so be careful not to overcook — the bread can become tough and chewy. Heat breads until warm, not hot, and cheese just until it begins to melt. Follow these tips when adapting or creating your own sandwiches:

Arrange hot dogs and similar sandwiches like the spokes of a wheel.

☐ The best breads to use for warmed sandwiches are day-old, full-bodied breads such as rye and whole wheat, and breads rich in eggs and shortening, like French or Italian.

☐ Heat sandwiches on paper napkins, paper towels, or paper plates to absorb the steam and prevent sogginess. To prevent splattering, you can wrap each sandwich in a paper towel. Remove wrapping immediately after warming. It takes less than 1 minute to heat most sandwiches.

☐ Thin slices of meat heat more quickly and taste better than one thick slice.

☐ Moist fillings, such as that in a Sloppy Joe or a barbecued beef sandwich, should generally be heated separately from the rolls, to prevent sogginess.

☐ The browning dish can be used to enhance your grilled cheese or Reuben. Brown the buttered outer side of bread before inserting filling.

Soup converts well and easily to the microwave method. One never worries about scorching the bottom of the pot. Find a recipe here with the approximate density and volume of the family favorite or the new conventional recipe you want to try.

To increase the tenderness of dried beans, combine beans with required water in recipe. Cook, covered, on COOK cycle 30 to 40 minutes, or until liquid reaches a full, rolling boil. Set aside. Canned, precooked beans and packaged dry soup mixes are perfect substitutes if you wish to shorten the time. The following tips will help you obtain excellent results with your own recipes:

□ Be careful with milk-based liquids or large quantities, which can boil over quickly. Always select a large enough microproof container to prevent any boiling over, and fill individual cups no more than two-thirds full.

□ Soup is cooked covered. Use microproof casserole lids, waxed paper, or plastic wrap.

□ Cooking time varies with the volume of liquid and density of food in soup.

□ Remember that the microwave's brief cooking time results in less evaporation of liquid than stovetop simmering.

□ Start with one-quarter the time recommended in a conventional recipe and adjust as needed to complete cooking.

□ The temperature of the liquid before heating will make a difference in final heating time. Water cold from the tap or drinks from the refrigerator will take somewhat longer than hot tap water or any room temperature liquid.

□ You can use a microproof thermometer to check the temperature of soup. Most people prefer 150°F for soup.

COOKING GUIDE — CANNED SOUP
Use COOK cycle.

Soup	Amount	Time (minutes)	Special Notes
Broth	10¾ oz.	4 - 5	Use 1½-quart casserole
Cream Style:	10¾ oz.	5½ - 7	Use 1½-quart casserole
Tomato	26 oz.	9 - 11½	Use 2-quart casserole
Bean, Pea, or Mushroom	10¾ oz.	8 - 9	Use 1½-quart casserole
Undiluted chunk-style vegetable	10¾ oz.	3 - 4½	Use 1-quart casserole
	19 oz.	6 - 8	Use 1½-quart casserole

• Add milk or water as directed on can. Stir.
• Stir cream-style soup halfway through cooking time.
• Let stand, covered, 3 minutes before serving.

COOKING GUIDE — QUICK SOUP
Use COOK cycle.

Soup	Number of Envelopes	Time (minutes)	Special Notes
Instant soup 1¼-ounce envelope	1	2½ - 3	Use ⅔ cup water in 8-ounce mug.
	2	4 - 4½	Use ⅔ cup water per 8-ounce mug.
	4	8 - 9	Use ⅔ cup water per 8-ounce mug.
Soup mix 2¾-ounce envelope	1	10½ - 13½	Use 4 cups water in 2-quart casserole.

Eldorado Chili —————————————— 4 servings

Total Cooking Time: 38 to 44 minutes

1 pound lean ground beef
½ cup minced onion
½ cup chopped green pepper
1 clove garlic, minced
1 can (28 ounces) tomatoes, broken up, liquid reserved
1 can (15 ounces) kidney beans, undrained
½ cup broken spaghetti
1½ to 2 tablespoons chili powder
½ teaspoon cumin
½ teaspoon salt

Place ground beef in 3-quart microproof casserole; break up with fork. Add onion, green pepper, and garlic. Cover. Use COOK cycle and cook 8 to 9 minutes, stirring once during cooking time. Break up ground beef with fork; drain. Add remaining ingredients; mix lightly. Cover. Use COOK cycle and cook 30 to 35 minutes, or until spaghetti is cooked, stirring every 10 minutes during cooking time. Let stand 10 minutes before serving.

Creamy Clam Chowder —————— 4 to 6 servings

Total Cooking Time: 44 to 46 minutes

3 slices bacon, diced
2 medium potatoes, peeled, cut in ½-inch cubes
2 medium carrots, thinly sliced
1 medium onion, chopped
¼ cup butter or margarine
¼ cup all-purpose flour
2 cans (6½ ounces each) minced clams, liquid reserved
1 tablespoon minced fresh parsley
½ teaspoon salt
⅛ teaspoon white pepper
3 cups milk

Place bacon in 3-quart microproof casserole. Cover. Use COOK cycle and cook 7 minutes, or until crisp. Stir in onion, potatoes, and carrots. Use COOK cycle and cook 20 minutes, or until vegetables are tender.

Place butter in 2-cup glass measure. Use COOK cycle and cook 1 minute, or until melted. Stir flour into butter; add to vegetable mixture, blending thoroughly.

Add enough water to reserved clam liquid to equal 2 cups liquid. Stir liquid, parsley, salt, and pepper into casserole. Cover. Use COOK cycle and cook 6 to 8 minutes, or until hot, stirring once during cooking.

Stir in milk and clams. Use DEFROST cycle and cook 10 minutes, or until hot. Let stand 10 minutes before serving.

Split Pea and Ham Soup ———— 8 to 10 servings
Total Cooking Time: 75 to 85 minutes

8 cups water
1 smoked ham hock (1½ to
  2 pounds)
1 cup chopped onion
1 package (6 ounces) split
  pea soup mix
3 black peppercorns
1 clove garlic, minced
1 bay leaf
½ teaspoon salt
½ teaspoon white pepper

Combine all ingredients in 4-quart microproof casserole. Cover. Use COOK cycle and cook 70 to 80 minutes, or until peas are tender. Remove ham hock from soup; cool until ham hock can be handled and meat cut from bone. Add meat to soup. Discard peppercorns and bay leaf. Stir. Use COOK cycle and cook 5 minutes, or until heated through.

Hearty Tomato Soup ———— 6 servings
Total Cooking Time: 35 to 38 minutes

2 medium onions, chopped
3 tablespoons butter or
  margarine
1 can (28 ounces) tomatoes,
  broken up; liquid
  reserved
3 cups beef broth or
  bouillon
½ teaspoon salt
¼ teaspoon oregano
¼ teaspoon freshly ground
  pepper
Shredded Cheddar cheese

Combine onions and butter in 3-quart microproof casserole. Use COOK cycle and cook 15 to 18 minutes, or until onions are transparent, stirring once during cooking time. Add remaining ingredients, except cheese; stir. Cover. Use COOK cycle and cook 20 minutes, or until heated through. Let stand 10 minutes. Purée in container of electric blender or food processor. Serve in bowls sprinkled with Cheddar cheese.

If you'd like to cut about 300 calories from this recipe, substitute 3 tablespoons beef broth or bouillon for butter when cooking the onions.

Pumpkin Soup —————————— 6 to 8 servings

Total Cooking Time: 35 to 38 minutes

1/4 cup butter or margarine
1 cup chopped onions
4 cups chicken stock or
   broth, divided
1 can (16 ounces) pumpkin
2 cups milk
1 bay leaf
1/2 teaspoon sugar
1/4 teaspoon nutmeg
1/8 teaspoon white pepper
1/2 cup dairy sour cream
   Minced chives or thinly
   sliced green onions

Combine butter and onions in 3-quart microproof casserole. Cover. Use COOK cycle and cook 15 to 18 minutes, or until onions are transparent. Transfer to blender. Add 1 cup of the chicken stock; process until smooth. Return mixture to casserole. Stir in pumpkin, remaining 3 cups chicken stock, milk, bay leaf, sugar, nutmeg, and pepper. Cover. Use COOK cycle and cook 20 minutes, or until hot, stirring after 10 minutes. Discard bay leaf. Garnish individual servings with a dollop of sour cream and sprinkle with chives.

Tuna-Vegetable Soup —————— 3 to 4 servings

Total Cooking Time: 45 to 47 minutes

2 cups water
1 medium potato, peeled and
   sliced
1/4 cup chopped onion
1/4 cup diced carrot
1/4 cup sliced celery
1 teaspoon chopped chives
1 teaspoon Worcestershire
   sauce
1/2 teaspoon salt
3 cubes chicken bouillon
   Dash freshly ground
   pepper
3/4 cup fresh or frozen corn,
   (thaw, if frozen)
1 can (7 ounces) tuna,
   drained and flaked
1 cup light cream or
   half-and-half

In 3-quart microproof casserole, combine water, potato, onion, carrot, celery, chives, Worcestershire, salt, bouillon, and pepper. Cover. Use COOK cycle and cook 20 minutes, or until all vegetables are tender. Add corn. Cover. Use COOK cycle and cook 20 minutes, or until corn is tender. Stir in tuna and cream. Cover. Use DEFROST cycle and cook 5 to 7 minutes, or until heated through. Stir; let stand 5 minutes before serving.

To reduce calories, substitute 1 cup evaporated low-fat milk for 1 cup light cream.

Corn and Sausage Chowder —————— 8 servings
Total Cooking Time: 29 to 33 minutes

½ pound link pork sausage
1 small onion, chopped
¼ cup chopped green pepper
2 cans (17 ounces each) cream-style corn
2 cups milk
1 can (10¾ ounces) condensed cream of potato soup
3 teaspoons chopped pimiento
1 teaspoon salt
¼ teaspoon freshly ground pepper

Place sausage in 3-quart microproof casserole; cover with paper towels. Use COOK cycle and cook 8 to 10 minutes, or until no longer pink, rearranging once during cooking time. Remove sausages from casserole; set aside to cool, reserving 1 tablespoon drippings in casserole. Add onion and green pepper to drippings. Use COOK cycle and cook 2 minutes, or until onion is transparent. Slice sausages. Add sausages and remaining ingredients; stir to blend. Cover. Use COOK cycle and cook 19 to 21 minutes, or until mixture boils, stirring once during cooking.

Quick Minestrone ————————————— 8 servings
Total Cooking Time: 48 to 50 minutes

2 cups cubed cooked beef or ham
1 can (16 ounces) tomatoes, broken up, liquid reserved
1 can (15 ounces) kidney beans, undrained
1 can (10¾ ounces) condensed tomato soup
1 cup water
1 cup shredded cabbage
½ cup uncooked vermicelli, broken in 1-inch pieces
1 clove garlic, minced
1 tablespoon Worcestershire sauce
½ teaspoon salt
½ teaspoon basil
¼ teaspoon freshly ground pepper
Grated Parmesan cheese

Combine all ingredients, except Parmesan cheese, in 3-quart microproof casserole. Cover. Use COOK cycle and cook 48 to 50 minutes, or until vermicelli is cooked, stirring twice during cooking time. Let stand 10 minutes. Serve in bowls sprinkled with Parmesan cheese.

Manhattan Seafood Chowder —— 5 to 6 servings
Total Cooking Time: 29 to 31 minutes

1 package (16 ounces) frozen
  cod, flounder or
  haddock fillets
2 tablespoons vegetable oil
1 medium green pepper,
  seeded and cut in
  thin strips
1 small onion, sliced
1 clove garlic, minced
1 can (16 ounces) tomatoes
1 bottle (8 ounces) clam juice
¼ teaspoon basil
¼ teaspoon salt
⅛ teaspoon white pepper
1 can (10 ounces) minced clams,
  undrained

Partially thaw frozen fish per instructions (page 131). Cut into chunks and set aside. In 3-quart microproof bowl, combine oil, green pepper, onion, and garlic. Cook on HI (max. power) 3 minutes, stirring once. Add fish, tomatoes, clam juice, basil, salt, and pepper. Cook on HI (max. power) 10 minutes. Add clams and liquid; stir. Cook on HI (max. power) 3 minutes, or until heated through and fish flakes easily.

Onion-Beef Soup ——————————— 6 servings
Total Cooking Time: 30 to 35 minutes

3 medium onions, thinly
  sliced
¼ cup butter or margarine
4 cups beef broth
1 teaspoon Worcestershire
  sauce
1 teaspoon salt
1 teaspoon soy sauce
½ teaspoon paprika
  Grated Parmesan cheese

Combine onions and butter in 3-quart microproof casserole. Cover. Use COOK cycle and cook 15 to 18 minutes, or until onions are transparent, stirring once during cooking time. Stir in remaining ingredients, except cheese. Use COOK cycle and cook 15 to 17 minutes, or until hot. Serve in bowls with cheese sprinkled on top.

Manhattan Seafood Chowder→

Beef Vegetable Soup —————— 8 servings
Total Cooking Time: 47 to 53 minutes

1 pound lean ground beef
4 cups water
1 can (16 ounces) tomatoes, broken up, liquid reserved
1 package (10 ounces) frozen mixed vegetables, thawed
1 cup uncooked noodles
1 envelope onion soup mix
1 bay leaf
1 teaspoon salt
⅛ teaspoon freshly ground pepper

Place ground beef in 3-quart microproof casserole; break up with fork. Use COOK cycle and cook 7 to 8 minutes, or until beef is no longer red, stirring once during cooking. Break up ground beef with fork; drain. Stir in remaining ingredients. Cover. Use COOK cycle and cook 40 to 45 minutes, or until mixture boils and noodles are cooked, stirring every 10 minutes. Let stand, covered, 10 minutes. Discard bay leaf before serving.

Lemon Chicken Rice Soup ————— 4 servings
Total Cooking Time: 37 minutes

4 cups chicken broth
¼ cup instant rice
3 eggs
3 tablespoons lemon juice
1 cup minced cooked chicken

Pour broth into 2-quart glass measure. Use COOK cycle and cook 25 minutes. Add rice. Cover and let stand 5 minutes. Beat eggs until foamy. Beat in lemon juice. Gradually add 1 cup hot broth to egg mixture, beating constantly. Stir egg mixture into remaining hot broth. Use DEFROST cycle and cook 10 minutes, or until soup is thickened, stirring every 2 minutes. Stir in chicken. Use DEFROST cycle and cook 2 minutes. Serve in bowls garnished with a lemon slice, if desired.

Hot Dog Cheese Wrap —————— 2 servings
Total Cooking Time: 3½ minutes

2 slices bacon
2 hot dog buns
1 tablespoon mustard
1 slice Cheddar cheese
2 hot dogs

Place bacon between 2 sheets of paper towels. Use COOK cycle and cook 1½ minutes, or until partially cooked. Split buns; spread with mustard; set aside. Cut cheese into 8¼-inch strips; divide cheese into 2 stacks. Cut each hot dog lengthwise in half, almost through. Lay cheese strips in slit. Wrap bacon strip around each hot dog. Place hot dogs in buns. Wrap each with paper towels or napkin. Use DEFROST cycle and cook 2 minutes. Let stand 1 minute before serving.

Any favorite cheese can be substituted for Cheddar cheese.

Beef Tacos and Fixin's —————— 8 servings
Total Cooking Time: 11 minutes

1 pound lean ground beef
½ cup chopped onion
1 clove garlic, minced
½ cup tomato juice
1 package (1¼ ounces) taco seasoning mix
8 taco shells
2 cups shredded lettuce
2 medium tomatoes, chopped
1½ cups shredded Cheddar cheese
1 medium onion, finely chopped
1 avocado, diced

Place beef in 2-quart microproof casserole; break up with fork. Add onion and garlic. Use COOK cycle and cook 6 minutes, or until beef is no longer red, stirring several times during cooking time; drain. Stir in juice and taco seasoning. Use COOK cycle and cook 4 minutes, or until heated through. Arrange taco shells on microproof plate. Use COOK cycle and cook 1 minute. Divide beef mixture, lettuce, tomatoes, cheese, onion, and avocado among shells. Serve with a favorite hot sauce, if desired.

Triple Decker Favorite —————————— 1 serving
Total Cooking Time: 2 minutes

Butter or margarine
2 slices white bread, toasted
1 slice chicken
  Salt
  Freshly ground pepper
1 slice bacon, cooked until
  crisp (Guide, page 101)
  Mayonnaise
1 slice whole wheat bread,
  toasted
  Mustard
1 slice Swiss cheese
1 medium tomato, sliced

Butter white toast on 1 side. Place chicken on 1 slice toast; sprinkle with salt and pepper. Break bacon in half and place on chicken. Spread mayonnaise on 1 side of whole wheat toast. Place whole wheat toast, mayonnaise side down, on top of bacon. Spread top of whole wheat toast with mustard. Add Swiss cheese and tomato slices. Sprinkle with salt and pepper. Top with remaining toast, buttered side down. Wrap sandwich in paper napkin and place on microproof plate. Use DEFROST cycle and cook 2 minutes, or until cheese is melted and sandwich is warm. Cut in half to serve.

Two sandwiches can be cooked at the same time. Double cooking time.

Barbecued Beef —————————— 2 servings
Total Cooking Time: 2½ to 3½ minutes

1 cup shredded cooked
  roast beef
3 tablespoons catsup
½ envelope onion soup mix
  Dash Worcestershire sauce
2 hamburger buns, split

Combine all ingredients, except buns, in 1½-quart microproof casserole. Cover. Use COOK cycle and cook 2 to 2½ minutes, or until heated through, stirring once during cooking time. Spoon mixture onto bottoms of buns; cover with tops. Place on paper towel-lined microproof plate. Use DEFROST cycle and cook 30 to 60 seconds, or until buns are warm.

Lemon Chicken Rice Soup (page 54), Triple Decker Favorite→

Super Sandwich ———————————————— 1 serving
Total Cooking Time: 3 to 4 minutes

1 slice (1-inch thick)
   Italian bread or 1
   large hard-roll, split
1 tablespoon butter or
   margarine
1 slice bologna
1 slice summer sausage
⅓ cup sauerkraut, drained
1 slice mozzarella cheese
   Paprika

Spread bread with butter. Cut bologna
and sausage in half. Place meat slices
alternately on bread. Top with
sauerkraut. Sprinkle with cheese. Place
sandwich on paper towel-lined
microproof plate. Use DEFROST cycle
and cook 3 to 4 minutes, or until cheese
is melted and sandwich is heated
through. Sprinkle with paprika. Let stand
1 minute before serving.

*To heat 4 sandwiches, arrange in circle
on plate. Use DEFROST cycle and cook
10 to 12 minutes.*

Hoboburgers ———————————————— 8 servings
Total Cooking Time: 14 minutes

1 pound lean ground beef
½ cup chopped onion
¼ cup chopped green pepper
1 can (6 ounces) tomato
   paste
1 can (15 ounces) kidney
   beans, drained
1 teaspoon salt
⅛ teaspoon freshly ground
   pepper
8 hamburger buns, toasted

Combine beef, onion, and green pepper
in 2-quart microproof casserole. Use
COOK cycle and cook 6 minutes, or
until beef is no longer red, stirring once
during cooking time. Break up beef with
fork; drain. Add remaining ingredients,
except buns. Blend well. Cover. Use
COOK cycle and cook 8 minutes,
stirring twice during cooking time.
Spoon onto bottoms of hamburger buns;
cover with tops.

Cheeseburger —————————— 4 servings
Total Cooking Time: 7 to 9 minutes

1 pound lean ground beef
Garlic salt
Freshly ground pepper
4 hamburger buns, split and toasted
4 slices process American cheese

Season ground beef with garlic salt and pepper. Shape into 4 patties. Arrange in 10-inch round microproof baking dish. Cover with waxed paper. Use COOK cycle and cook 3 minutes. Turn patties over; season. Cover. Use COOK cycle and cook 3 to 4 minutes, or until desired degree of doneness.

Place patties on bottoms of hamburger buns. Top each with slice of cheese. Place cheeseburgers in a circle on 10-inch paper towel-lined microproof plate. Use COOK cycle and cook 1 to 2 minutes, or until cheese is melted. Cover with tops of buns. Let stand 1 minute before serving.

Ranchburgers —————————— 4 servings
Total Cooking Time: 11 to 12 minutes

1 cup sauerkraut, drained
½ cup cranberry sauce
¼ cup chili sauce or catsup
1 tablespoon brown sugar
4 onion rolls, split
1 pound lean ground beef
½ envelope onion soup mix

Combine sauerkraut, cranberry sauce, chili sauce, and brown sugar in 4-cup glass measure; mix well. Use COOK cycle and cook 5 minutes, stirring once during cooking. Cover and set aside.

Combine ground beef and soup mix; blend thoroughly. Shape into 4 patties. Arrange in 10-inch round microproof baking dish. Cover with waxed paper. Use COOK cycle and cook 3 minutes. Turn patties over; cover. Use COOK cycle and cook 3 to 4 minutes, or until desired degree of doneness.

Place patties on bottoms of rolls. Top with hot sauerkraut mixture. Cover with tops of rolls.

Tuna, Tomato, and Cheese ———— 6 servings
Total Cooking Time: 7 to 8 minutes

3 English muffins, split
  and toasted
3 tablespoons butter or
  margarine
1 large tomato, cut in
  6 slices
1 can (6½ ounces) tuna,
  drained and flaked
2 tablespoons mayonnaise
3 slices Cheddar or Swiss
  cheese

Spread muffins with butter. Arrange in circle on large paper towel-lined microproof plate. Place tomato slice on each muffin. Mix tuna and mayonnaise until blended. Divide and spoon tuna over tomato slices. Cut cheese diagonally in half to form triangles. Place 1 triangle of cheese on each muffin. Use DEFROST cycle and cook 7 to 8 minutes, or until cheese is melted and muffin topping is warm. Let stand 2 minutes before serving.

A single split muffin can be prepared and cooked on DEFROST cycle for 1 to 1½ minutes. Toasted bread can be substituted for English muffins.

Mushrooms Benedict ———— 4 servings
Total Cooking Time: 6 to 7 minutes

1 cup (4 ounces) sliced
  mushrooms
1 tablespoon butter or
  margarine
⅓ cup water
3 teaspoons all-purpose
  flour
½ teaspoon instant beef
  bouillon granules
½ teaspoon Worcestershire
  sauce
¼ cup dairy sour cream
1 teaspoon parsley flakes
2 English muffins, split
  and toasted
4 slices cooked ham

In 2-cup glass measure, combine mushrooms and butter. Use COOK cycle and cook 2½ to 3 minutes, or until tender, stirring once during cooking time. Use slotted spoon to remove mushrooms; set aside; reserve liquid. In small microproof bowl, blend water, flour, bouillon, and Worcestershire; stir into mushroom liquid. Use COOK cycle and cook 1½ to 2 minutes, or until thickened, stirring once during cooking. Stir in sour cream, parsley, and mushrooms.

Place muffins on paper towel-lined microproof plate. Place a slice of ham on each muffin half. Use DEFROST cycle and cook 2 minutes, or until ham is heated through. Remove to serving plate. Top each with ¼ cup mushroom sauce. Serve immediately.

A LA CARTE

sparagus and broccoli, arranged
r cooking. Split the broccoli stalks
ight). Use DEFROST cycle and
ook 1 minute to warm cheese. Use
OOK cycle and cook 1 minute to
elt cheese (above).

Here's where you'll find all the special side dishes that help make a banquet out of any entrée. You'll also discover the microwave way for "special order" and traditional egg or cheese dishes.

Vegetables and the microwave oven were made for each other, or so you'll think when you sit down with one of these dishes on the table. Just think — little water, and sometimes none at all, is used in cooking vegetables. They don't lose any vitamins and keep just-picked flavor and color.

Potatoes? You bet. There's no more dramatic example of microwave cooking speed than a baked potato that took all of 6 to 8 minutes to cook!

But, let's face it, nothing is absolutely perfect. Pasta and rice cook fine in the microwave but no time is saved. That's because they must be reconstituted and there's no way to shorten the conventional timing. They do reheat incredibly well, however.

Converting Your Recipes

As you convert, consider that vegetables are at their best when served crisp-tender, as in wok cooking. For a softer texture, however, simply add a bit more water and increase cooking time until they reach the texture you prefer. All vegetables use the COOK cycle. To convert that family favorite, simply find a similar recipe here or look for timing hints in the Guides.

☐ You can use a microproof thermometer when cooking most vegetable dishes. 150°F is the usually preferred temperature for doneness.

☐ Pasta, rice, and cereals are best when added to other ingredients, as in vegetable, meat, or cheese casseroles. While the oven can cook them separately, there's no advantage. It is wise to reheat them in the oven, however. You add no water and they are like fresh cooked. Use the COOK cycle and cook 4 to 5 minutes for 1 cup (cooked), 6 to 7 minutes for 2 cups, etc. Cover tightly.

☐ Grits or other hot cereals are interesting side dishes for brunch, cooked in individual bowls. Use the COOK cycle and cook 8 to 9 minutes for ⅓ cup grits (uncooked); 2 to 3 minutes for ⅓ cup quick oatmeal. Follow package directions for liquid.

☐ To reheat mashed potatoes, use the COOK cycle and cook 3 to 3½ minutes.

☐ Eggs are undercooked slightly and allowed to complete cooking during standing time. Eggs are cooked covered to trap steam and assure even cooking.

Cut carrots diagonally to expose more area for faster cooking. It's also a bit more attractive. Cut all vegetables uniformly when possible.

COOKING GUIDE — SCRAMBLED EGGS
Use COOK cycle.

Number of Eggs	Liquid (Milk or Cream)	Butter	Minutes to Cook
1	1 tablespoon	1 teaspoon	1 to 1½
2	2 tablespoons	2 teaspoons	2 to 2½
4	3 tablespoons	3 teaspoons	4½ to 5½
6	4 tablespoons	4 teaspoons	7 to 8

• Break eggs into a microproof bowl or glass measure. Add milk or cream. Beat with a fork. Add butter. Cover with waxed paper. Stir at least once during cooking from the outside to the center. Let stand 1 minute before serving.

COOKING GUIDE — POACHED EGGS
Use COOK cycle.

Number of Eggs	Water	Container	Minutes to Boil Water	Minutes to Cook
1	¼ cup	6-ounce microproof custard cup	1¾ to 2¾	1
2	¼ cup	6-ounce microproof custard cups	2¾	1½ to 2
3	¼ cup	6-ounce microproof custard cups	2¾ to 3¼	2 to 2¼
4	1 cup	1-quart microproof dish	2¼ to 4¼	2½ to 3

• Bring water to a boil with a pinch of salt and up to ¼ teaspoon vinegar. Break egg carefully into hot water. Pierce egg lightly with toothpick. Cover with waxed paper. Let stand, covered, 1 minute before serving.

COOKING GUIDE — RICE
Use COOK cycle.

Food	Amount Uncooked	Water	Minutes to Full Boil	Time (minutes)	Standing Time (minutes)	Special Notes
Short-grain	1 cup	2 cups	6 - 6½	11 - 15	5	2-quart casserole
Long-grain	1 cup	2 cups	6 - 6½	13 - 17	5	2-quart casserole
Wild rice	1 cup	3 cups	9 - 10	30 - 40	5	3-quart casserole
Brown rice	1 cup	3 cups	9 - 10	35 - 40	5	3-quart casserole
Quick-cooking	1 cup	1 cup	3½ - 4	0	5	1-quart casserole

• Add salt and butter or margarine according to package directions. Cover tightly. Let stand, covered, 5 minutes before serving.

Vegetable Cooking Tips

1. Choose a wide, shallow dish so vegetables can be spread out.
2. Cover all vegetables tightly.
3. Pouches of frozen vegetables require steam vents. Slit pouch and cook on micro-proof dish.
4. Frozen vegetables without sauces can be cooked in their cartons without water. Remove waxed paper wrap-ping before placing carton in oven. (Remove frozen-in-sauce vegetables if they are packaged in cartons rather than pouches. Place in 1½-quart microproof casserole. Add liquid before cooking according to package directions.)
5. After cooking, allow all vegetables to stand, covered, 2 to-3 minutes.

COOKING GUIDE — VEGETABLES
Use COOK cycle.

Food	Amount	Vegetable Preparation	Time (minutes)	Water	Special Notes
Artichokes 3½" in diameter ½ lb. (med)	Fresh: 1 2	Wash thoroughly. Cut tops off each leaf.	8 - 10 12 - 14	¼ cup ½ cup	When done, a leaf peeled from whole comes off easily.
	Frozen: 10 oz.	Slit pouch.	6 - 7½		
Asparagus: spears and cut pieces	Fresh: 1 lb. Frozen: 10 oz.	Wash thoroughly. Snap off tough base and discard.	2½ - 3½ 9 - 10	¼ cup None	Stir or rearrange once during cooking time.
Beans: green, wax, French-cut	Fresh: 1 lb. Frozen: 6 oz.	Remove ends. Wash. well. Leave whole or break in pieces.	12 - 14 9 - 11	¼ cup None	Stir once or rearrange as necessary.
Beets	4 medium	Scrub beets. Leave 1" of top on beet.	19 - 22	¼ cup	After cooking, peel. Cut or leave whole.
Broccoli	Fresh, whole, 1-1½ lbs. Frozen, whole Fresh, chopped, 1-1½ lbs. Frozen, chopped 10 oz.	Remove outer leaves. Slit stalks.	11 - 13 10 - 11½ 10 - 11 9½ - 11	¼ cup ¼ cup ¼ cup None	Stir or rearrange during cooking time.
Brussels sprouts	Fresh: 1 lb. Frozen: 10 oz.	Remove outside leaves if wilted. Cut off stems. Wash.	10 - 12 8 - 10	¼ cup None	Stir or rearrange once during cooking time.
Cabbage	½ medium head, shredded 1 medium head, wedges	Remove outside wilted leaves.	6 - 7½ 14 - 16	¼ cup ¼ cup	Rearrange wedges after 7 minutes.

Food	Amount	Vegetable Preparation	Time (minutes)	Water	Special Notes
Carrots	4: sliced or diced	Peel and cut off tops.	8 - 10	1 Tb.	Stir once during cooking time.
	6: sliced or diced	Fresh young carrots cook best.	11 - 13	2 Tbs.	
	8 tiny, whole		11 - 13	2 Tbs.	
	Frozen: 10 oz.		10 - 11½	None	
Cauliflower	1 medium, in florets	Cut tough stem. Wash, remove outside leaves.	10 - 12	¼ cup	Stir after 5 minutes.
	1 medium, whole	Remove core.	11 - 13	¼ cup	Turn over once.
	Frozen: 10 oz.		10 - 11½	¼ cup	
Celery	2½ cups, 1″ slices	Clean stalks thoroughly.	10 - 11	¼ cup	Stir after 5 minutes.
Corn: kernel	Frozen: 10 oz.		7 - 8	¼ cup	Stir halfway through cooking time.
On the cob	1 ear	Husk, wrap each	5 - 6	None	Rearrange halfway
	2 ears	in waxed paper. Place	7 - 8	None	through cooking time
	3 ears	on glass tray in oven.	10 - 12	None	unless cooked on
	4 ears	Cook no more than 4 at a time.	13 - 15	None	microproof rack.
	Frozen,	Flat dish, covered.		None	Rearrange halfway
	2 ears		7 - 8½	None	through cooking time
	4 ears		12 - 14	None	
Eggplant	1 medium, sliced	Wash and peel. Cut into slices or cubes.	6½ - 8	2 Tbs.	
	1 medium, whole	Pierce skin.	7½ - 9		Place on micro-proof rack.
Greens: collard, kale, etc.	Fresh: 1 lb.	Wash. Remove wilted leaves or tough stem.	8½ - 10	None	
	Frozen: 10 oz.		9 - 10	None	
Mushrooms	Fresh: ½ lb., sliced	Add butter or water.	3 - 4	2 Tbs.	Stir halfway through cooking time.
Okra	Fresh: ½ lb.	Wash thoroughly. Leave whole or cut	4 - 6	¼ cup	
	Frozen: 10 oz.	in thick slices.	9 - 10	None	
Onions	1 lb., tiny whole	Peel. Add 1 Tb. butter.	8 - 10	¼ cup	Stir once during cooking time.
	1 lb., medium to large	Peel and quarter. Add 1 Tb. butter.	9 - 11	¼ cup	
Parsnips	4 medium, quartered	Peel and cut.	10 - 12	¼ cup	Stir once during cooking time.
Peas: green	Fresh: 1 lb.	Shell peas. Rinse well.	9 - 10	¼ cup	Stir once during cooking time.
	Fresh: 2 lbs.		10 - 11	½ cup	
	Frozen: 6 oz.		6 - 7½	None	
Peas and onions	Frozen: 10 oz.		7½ - 10	2 Tbs.	
Pea pods	Frozen: 6 oz.		4 - 5½	2 Tbs.	
Potatoes, sweet 5 - 6 oz. ea.	1	Scrub well. Pierce with fork. Place on rack or paper towel in circle, 1″ apart.	5 - 6	None	
	2		7½ - 9	None	
	4		10 - 13	None	
	6		13 - 16	None	

Cooking Guide for Vegetables is continued on next page→

Food	Amount	Vegetable Preparation	Time (minutes)	Water	Special Notes
Potatoes, white baking 6 - 8 oz. ea.	1 2 3 4 5	Wash and scrub well. Pierce with fork. Place on rack or paper towel in circle, 1″ apart.	6 - 8 8 - 10 11 - 15 14 - 18 19 - 22	None None None None None	
russet, boiling	3	Peel potatoes, cut in quarters.	14 - 17	½ cup	Stir once during cooking time.
Rutabaga	Fresh: 1 lb. Frozen: 10 oz.	Wash well. Remove tough stems or any wilted leaves.	7½ - 9 9 - 10	None None	Stir once during cooking time.
Spinach	Fresh: 1 lb. Frozen: 10 oz.	Wash well. Remove tough stems. Drain.	8 - 9½ 9 - 10	None None	Stir once during cooking time.
Squash, acorn or butternut	1 - 1½ lbs. whole	Scrub. Pierce with fork.	13 - 16		Cut and remove seeds to serve.
Spaghetti squash	2 - 3 lbs.	Scrub, pierce. Place on rack.	8 per lb.	None	Serve with butter, Parmesan cheese, or spaghetti sauce. Let stand 5 minutes.
Turnips	4 cups cubed	Peel, wash.	12 - 15	¼ cup	Stir after 5 minutes.
Zucchini	3 cups, sliced	Wash; do not peel.	6 - 7	¼ cup	Stir after 4 minutes.

COOKING GUIDE — CONVENIENCE VEGETABLES
Use COOK cycle.

Food	Amount	Time (minutes)	Special Notes
Au gratin vegetables, frozen	11½ oz.	11 - 13	Use glass loaf dish, covered.
Baked beans, frozen	6 oz.	9 - 11	Use 1½-quart casserole, covered. Stir once.
Corn, scalloped frozen	12 oz.	8 - 9	Use 1-quart casserole, covered.
Potatoes stuffed, frozen	2	11 - 14	Use shallow dish. Cover with waxed paper.
Tots, frozen	16 oz. 32 oz.	10 - 12 14 - 17	Use 2-quart round or oval baking dish. Rearrange once.
Creamed potato mix	4 - 5 oz.	23 - 28	
Au gratin, frozen	11½ oz.	15	Use 1½-quart casserole, covered with waxed paper.
Instant mashed	3½ oz. packet	6 - 8	Use covered casserole. Follow package directions. Reduce liquid by 1 tablespoon.
Peas, pea pods, chestnuts, frozen	10 oz.	7½ - 9	Place pouch on plate. Slit pouch. Flex once during cooking time to mix.
Stuffing mix	6 oz.	10 - 11	Use 1½-quart casserole, covered. Follow package directions.

COOKING GUIDE — CANNED VEGETABLES
Use COOK cycle.

Size	Minutes Drained	Minutes Undrained	Special Notes
8 ounces 15 ounces 17 ounces	2 - 2½ 3 - 3½ 4 - 5	2½ - 3 3½ - 5 5 - 6	Regardless of quantity: use a 4-cup microproof casserole. covered. Stir once. Let stand, covered, 2 - 3 minutes before serving.

The Blanching Guide

The microwave oven can be a valuable and appreciated aid in preparing fresh vegetables for the freezer. (The oven is, however, *not* recommended for canning.) Here are some tips in preparing vegetables for blanching:

☐ Measure amounts to be blanched; place by batches, in microproof casserole.
☐ Cover and use COOK cycle for time indicated on chart.
☐ Stir vegetables halfway through cooking.
☐ Let vegetables stand, covered, 1 minute after cooking.
☐ Place vegetables in ice water at once to stop cooking. When vegetables feel cool, spread on towel to absorb excess moisture.
☐ Package in freezer containers or pouches. Seal, label, date, and freeze.

BLANCHING GUIDE — VEGETABLES
Use COOK cycle.

Food	Amount	Water	Approximate Time (minutes)	Casserole Size
Asparagus (cut in 1-inch pieces)	4 cups	¼ cup	6	1½ quart
Beans, green or wax (cut in 1-inch pieces)	1 pound	½ cup	6½ - 7	1½ quart
Broccoli (cut in 1-inch pieces)	1 pound	⅓ cup	8	1½ quart
Carrots (sliced)	1 pound	⅓ cup	8	1½ quart
Cauliflower (cut in florets)	1 head	⅓ cup	8	2 quart
Corn (cut from cob)	4 cups	none	5½	1½ quart
Corn-on-the-cob (husked)	6 ears	none	7	1½ quart
Onion (quartered)	4 medium	½ cup	4 - 6	1 quart
Parsnips (cubed)	1 pound	¼ cup	3½ - 5½	1½ quart
Peas (shelled)	4 cups	¼ cup	6	1½ quart
Snow peas	4 cups	¼ cup	4½ - 5	1½ quart
Spinach (washed)	1 pound	none	5½	2 quart
Turnips (cubed)	1 pound	¼ cup	4 - 6	1½ quart
Zucchini (sliced or cubed)	1 pound	¼ cup	5½	1½ quart

Acorn Squash with Peas —————— 4 servings

Total Cooking Time: 27 to 29 minutes

2 acorn squash (1 to 1½
   pounds each)
1 package (10 ounces)
   frozen peas
Salt
Freshly ground pepper
1 jar (4 ounces) pimiento,
   drained
1 tablespoon butter or
   margarine

Cook acorn squash according to Guide (page 66). Place package of peas on microproof plate. Use DEFROST cycle and cook 6 to 8 minutes, or until thawed and warm. While peas are thawing, cut squash in half lengthwise; scoop out seeds. Place cut-side up on microproof plate. Sprinkle each half with salt and pepper. In small dish, mix peas, pimiento, and butter. Divide among squash halves. Use COOK cycle and cook 1 minute. Serve hot.

Spinach with Cheese —————— 6 to 8 servings

Total Cooking Time: 29½ to 34 minutes

1 package (10 ounces) frozen
   chopped spinach
1 cup White Sauce (page 73)
¼ teaspoon onion salt
⅛ teaspoon freshly ground
   pepper
2 large eggs, separated
3 slices Cheddar cheese,
   cut diagonally in half

Place unopened package of spinach on microproof plate. Use COOK cycle and cook 9 minutes; drain. Squeeze all moisture from spinach.

Prepare White Sauce in 4-quart glass measure. Stir in spinach, salt, and pepper; set aside.

In mixing bowl, beat egg whites until stiff, but not dry; set aside. In another mixing bowl, beat egg yolks. Add yolks to spinach mixture; stir gently to blend. Carefully fold in egg whites. Pour into 9-inch round microproof dish. Smooth top with spatula. Use DEFROST cycle and cook 12 to 16 minutes, or until center is set, rotating dish if cooking unevenly.

Arrange cheese triangles around outside of dish with points toward center. Cover with aluminum foil. Let stand 3 minutes to soften cheese.

Acorn Squash with Peas→

Carrot and Basil Bake —————————— 6 servings
Total Cooking Time: 15 to 17 minutes

1 pound carrots, peeled and
   shredded
1 small onion, minced
2 tablespoons butter or
   margarine
2 tablespoons water
1 teaspoon parsley flakes
½ teaspoon salt
½ teaspoon crushed sweet
   basil

Combine all ingredients in 1¾-quart microproof casserole. Cover. Use COOK cycle and cook 15 to 17 minutes, stirring twice during cooking time. Let stand 3 minutes before serving.

String Beans and Pearl Onions ————— 7 servings
Total Cooking Time: 19 to 21 minutes

1 package (9 ounces) frozen
   whole green beans
1 package (10 ounces) frozen
   pearl onions in cream
   sauce, removed from pouch
⅛ teaspoon summer savory

Place green beans in 1¾-quart microproof casserole. Place onions in cream sauce over beans. Sprinkle with savory. Use DEFROST cycle and cook 7 minutes, stirring once during cooking. Use COOK cycle and cook 12 to 14 minutes, or until crisp-tender. Let stand 3 minutes before serving.

If you prefer, substitute 2 tablespoons pimiento for the onions. Reduce cooking time by 4 minutes.

Braised Celery and Peas —————— 6 servings
Total Cooking Time: 18 to 22 minutes

2 cups sliced celery, ¼
   inch thick
⅓ cup chopped onion
2 tablespoons butter or
   margarine
2 tablespoons water
½ teaspoon salt
¼ teaspoon celery salt
1 package (10 ounces)
   frozen peas
1 tablespoon minced fresh
   parsley

In 2-quart microproof casserole, combine celery, onion, butter, water, salt, and celery salt. Cover. Use COOK cycle and cook 10 to 12 minutes, or until vegetables are tender, stirring once during cooking. Add peas. Cover. Use COOK cycle and cook 8 to 10 minutes, stirring after 4 minutes. Sprinkle with parsley before serving.

Garden Goodness ———————————— 6 servings

Total Cooking Time: 25 minutes

2 tablespoons butter or
   margarine
1 cup pearl onions,
   peeled
1 pound small new potatoes,
   washed
6 small carrots, peeled and
   cut into 1-inch pieces
1/3 cup water
1 tablespoon instant chicken
   bouillon granules
1/2 teaspoon salt
1 cup fresh or frozen peas
2 tablespoons minced parsley

Combine butter and onions in 2-quart microproof casserole. Cover. Use COOK cycle and cook 5 minutes. Add potatoes, carrots, water, bouillon, and salt. Use COOK cycle and cook 15 minutes, stirring once during cooking. Add peas. Cover. Use COOK cycle and cook 5 minutes, or until vegetables are crisp-tender. Stir in parsley. Cover and let stand 5 minutes before serving.

Green Beans with Bacon ————————— 4 servings

Total Cooking Time: 27 to 28 minutes

2 slices bacon
1/3 cup chopped onion
1 pound fresh green beans,
   trimmed and cut in
   1-inch pieces

Cut bacon into small pieces; place in 2-quart microproof casserole. Add onion. Cover. Use COOK cycle and cook 9 minutes, or until bacon is brown and onion transparent. Add beans. Cover. Use COOK cycle and cook 18 to 19 minutes, or until beans are tender, stirring twice during cooking time. Let stand 3 minutes before serving.

Norwegian Red Cabbage ———————— 4 servings

Total Cooking Time: 35 minutes

1 small head (1 to 1 1/2
   pounds) red cabbage,
   shredded
1/3 cup currant jelly
1/4 cup water
3 tablespoons vinegar
2 tablespoons butter or
   margarine
1/2 teaspoon salt
1/4 teaspoon caraway seed

Place cabbage in 3-quart microproof casserole. Add remaining ingredients; stir lightly to mix. Cover. Use COOK cycle and cook 5 minutes. Stir carefully; cover. Use COOK cycle and cook 30 minutes, or until cabbage is tender, stirring twice during cooking time.

Asparagus with Mustard Sauce ⸻ 6 servings
Total Cooking Time: 7 to 9 minutes

1½ pounds asparagus, cleaned
    and cut in pieces
¼ cup water
⅓ cup mayonnaise
1 tablespoon minced fresh
    parsley
1 teaspoon prepared mustard
½ teaspoon onion salt
⅛ teaspoon white pepper

In 2-quart microproof casserole, combine asparagus and water. Cover. Use COOK cycle and cook 6 to 7 minutes, or until tender, stirring once during cooking time; drain. Combine remaining ingredients, mixing lightly to coat asparagus. Use COOK cycle and cook 1 to 2 minutes, or until heated through.

Two packages (9 ounces each) frozen cut asparagus can be substituted for fresh asparagus; omit water.

Three Bean Bake ⸻ 8 to 10 servings
Total Cooking Time: 28 to 29 minutes

2 slices bacon, diced
1 small onion, chopped
1 can (31 ounces) pork and
    beans in tomato sauce
1 can (17 ounces) lima
    beans, drained
1 can (16 ounces) cut green
    beans, drained
¼ cup catsup
1 tablespoon prepared
    mustard

Place bacon in 2-quart microproof casserole. Cover. Use COOK cycle and cook 3 to 4 minutes, or until crisp. Remove bacon; set aside, reserving drippings. Stir onion into drippings. Cover. Use COOK cycle and cook 5 minutes, or until tender, stirring once during cooking. Add remaining ingredients; stir. Cover. Use COOK cycle and cook 20 minutes. Top with reserved bacon and serve.

Corn-in-the-Husk ⸻ 4 servings
Total Cooking Time: 16 to 18 minutes

4 ears corn in husks
    Butter or margarine
    Salt
    Freshly ground pepper

Discard soiled outer portion of husk. Soak corn in cold water 10 minutes. Drain, but do not dry. Arrange corn in spoke fashion on microproof plate. Use COOK cycle and cook 16 to 18 minutes, rearranging halfway through cooking time. Let stand 3 minutes. Peel and discard husks and silk. Serve with butter, salt, and pepper.

Broccoli and Sour Cream ———— 6 to 8 servings
Total Cooking Time: 21 to 23 minutes

1 package (18 ounces)
   frozen cut broccoli
2 tablespoons chopped onion
1 tablespoon water
1 tablespoon butter or
   margarine
1 cup dairy sour cream
½ teaspoon celery salt
¼ teaspoon celery seed
⅛ teaspoon white pepper

In 2-quart microproof casserole, combine broccoli, onion, water, and butter. Use COOK cycle and cook 21 to 23 minutes, or until vegetables are tender, stirring once during cooking time. Drain, if necessary. Combine remaining ingredients; stir into broccoli. Cover and let stand 3 minutes before serving.

Creamed Cabbage ———————— 6 servings
Total Cooking Time: 9 to 10 minutes

1 teaspoon cornstarch
½ cup milk
6 cups shredded cabbage
1 package (3 ounces) cream
   cheese, cut up
1 tablespoon parsley flakes
1 tablespoon minced onion
1 teaspoon salt
⅛ teaspoon white pepper

Dissolve cornstarch in milk. Combine all ingredients in 2-quart microproof casserole. Cover. Use COOK cycle and cook 9 to 10 minutes, or until cabbage is tender, stirring once during cooking time. Stir and let stand 2 minutes before serving.

White Sauce ————————————— 1 cup
Total Cooking Time: 8½ to 9 minutes

1 cup milk
2 tablespoons butter or
   margarine
2 tablespoons all-purpose
   flour
Dash white pepper
Dash grated or ground nutmeg

Pour milk into 2-cup glass measure. Use COOK cycle and cook 2 minutes; set aside. Place butter in 2-cup glass measure. Use COOK cycle and cook 1 minute, or until melted. Stir in flour. Use COOK cycle and cook 1 minute. Briskly stir in warm milk, pepper, and nutmeg. Use COOK cycle and cook 4½ to 5 minutes, or until mixture boils, stirring once during cooking time. Let stand 5 minutes before serving.

For Cheese Sauce, stir ½ to 1 cup shredded cheese into hot sauce until melted.

Potatoes Au Gratin ——————— 4 to 5 servings
Total Cooking Time: 15 to 16 minutes

1 package (16 ounces) frozen
   Southern-style hashed
   brown potatoes
1 can (10¾ ounces)
   condensed cream of
   potato soup
½ cup dairy sour cream
¾ cup shredded Cheddar
   cheese, divided

In 1¾-quart shallow microproof casserole, combine potatoes, soup, sour cream, and ½ cup cheese; blend well. Use COOK cycle and cook 15 to 16 minutes, or until potatoes are tender, stirring once during cooking time. Sprinkle with remaining ¼ cup cheese. Cover and let stand 3 minutes, or until cheese is melted.

Sliced Oven Fries ——————— 4 servings
Total Cooking Time: 15 to 20 minutes

4 medium potatoes, peeled
   and sliced
1 medium onion, sliced
1 teaspoon salt
   Dash freshly ground
   pepper
3 tablespoons butter or
   margarine
   Paprika

Combine potatoes, onion, salt, and pepper in shallow 1-quart microproof casserole. Dot with butter. Cover. Use COOK cycle and cook 15 to 20 minutes, or until potatoes are tender, stirring every 5 minutes. Sprinkle with paprika before serving.

Parslied Potatoes ——————— 4 to 6 servings
Total Cooking Time: 18 to 21 minutes

4 medium potatoes
¼ cup water
3 tablespoons butter or
   margarine
3 to 4 tablespoons minced
   fresh parsley
   Salt
   Freshly ground pepper

Peel potatoes and quarter. Combine potatoes and water in 2-quart microproof casserole; cover. Use COOK cycle and cook 18 to 21 minutes, or until tender, stirring once during cooking time; drain. Add butter, parsley, salt, and pepper. Stir until butter is melted. Serve immediately.

You may choose to use 16 whole new potatoes instead of quartering the larger variety.

Potato Boats ———————————— 4 servings

Total Cooking Time: 18 to 19 minutes

4 medium potatoes (5 to 6
   ounces each)
½ cup dairy sour cream
⅓ cup milk
3 tablespoons butter or
   margarine, cut up
2 tablespoons chopped chives
1 teaspoon salt
⅛ teaspoon freshly ground
   pepper
   Paprika

Arrange potatoes in a circular pattern on microproof plate. Use COOK cycle and cook 12 to 13 minutes, or until tender, turning potatoes over once during cooking. Let stand 5 minutes. Cut top one-third off potatoes. Scoop out pulp and place in mixing bowl, leaving ¼-inch thick shell. Mash potatoes. Beat in remaining ingredients, except paprika. Fill potato shells. Place on microproof plate. Sprinkle with paprika. Use COOK cycle and cook 6 minutes or until heated through.

Onion Pie in Rice Crust ———————— 6 servings

Total Cooking Time: 21 to 23 minutes

1 Rice Pie Crust (page 158)
1 cup shredded Cheddar
   cheese
1 cup shredded Swiss cheese
¼ cup thinly sliced green
   onion
1 tablespoon butter or
   margarine
1 can (13 ounces) evaporated
   milk
4 eggs
1 teaspoon prepared mustard
½ teaspoon salt
1 can (3 ounces) French-
   fried onions

Sprinkle cheeses in prepared pie crust. In 2-cup glass measure, combine onion and butter. Use COOK cycle and cook 3 minutes, or until onion is transparent, stirring after 1 minute. Add milk. Use COOK cycle and cook 3 minutes, or until milk is heated through.

In small bowl, combine eggs, mustard, and salt; mix lightly. Gradually pour hot milk mixture into egg mixture while beating. Pour carefully over cheese in pie crust. Crumble French-fried onions over top. Use COOK cycle and cook 15 to 17 minutes, or until center is nearly set, rotating dish if pie is cooking unevenly. Cover with aluminum foil; let stand on breadboard or heatproof counter top 10 minutes before serving.

German Potato Salad ———————— 5 to 6 servings
Total Cooking Time: 32½ to 38 minutes

4 large potatoes
4 slices bacon
1 medium onion, chopped
1 tablespoon all-purpose
   flour
½ cup water
¼ cup vinegar
¼ cup sugar
1 teaspoon salt
¾ teaspoon paprika
½ teaspoon celery seed
⅛ teaspoon freshly ground
   pepper

Cook potatoes according to Guide on page 66; set aside. Place bacon in 2-quart microproof casserole. Cover with paper toweling. Use COOK cycle and cook 7 to 9 minutes, or until crisp. Remove bacon from casserole; set aside. Reserve 4 tablespoons drippings. Add onion to drippings. Use COOK cycle and cook 2 minutes. Add flour; stir. Use COOK cycle and cook 1 minute, or until onion is transparent. Stir in remaining ingredients. Use COOK cycle and cook 4½ to 5 minutes, or until mixture thickens. Peel and slice potatoes. Add to hot mixture. Stir to coat potatoes with sauce. Crumble bacon over top. Serve warm.

If salad cools, reheat by using COOK cycle; cook 2 to 3 minutes.

Lemon-Glazed Carrots ———————— 4 to 5 servings
Total Cooking Time: 19 to 22 minutes

3 cups (about 10 medium)
   thinly sliced carrots
¼ cup water
¼ cup chopped green pepper
3 tablespoons butter or
   margarine
1 tablespoon lemon juice
½ teaspoon cornstarch
½ teaspoon sugar (optional)
¼ teaspoon grated lemon rind
¼ teaspoon salt
   Dash white pepper

In 1-quart microproof casserole, combine carrots and water. Cover. Use COOK cycle and cook 6 minutes. Stir in green pepper. Cover. Use COOK cycle and cook 12 to 15 minutes, or until carrots are tender, stirring once during cooking time. Drain. In small bowl, combine remaining ingredients; add to carrots. Stir until butter is melted. Use COOK cycle and cook 1 minute, or until sauce. is heated through.

Denver Scramble —————————————— 4 to 6 servings

Total Cooking Time: 6 to 7 minutes

4 eggs
1/4 cup mayonnaise
1/4 cup milk
1/2 cup minced cooked ham
1 tablespoon instant minced onion
1 tablespoon chopped pimiento
1 tablespoon chopped green pepper
1/8 teaspoon salt
1 small tomato, seeded and chopped
4 to 6 slices toast

Combine eggs, mayonnaise, and milk in 1- to 1 1/2-quart microproof casserole; blend well. Stir in ham, onion, pimiento, green pepper, and salt. Cover. Use COOK cycle and cook 5 to 6 minutes, or until just set, stirring every minute during cooking time. Stir in tomato. Use COOK cycle and cook covered 1 minute. Let stand 2 minutes. Serve with toast.

This recipe can be doubled and cooked in 2-quart microproof casserole. Double cooking time.

Eggs Florentine —————————————— 4 servings

Total Cooking Time: 30 to 35 minutes

1/2 package (12 ounces) frozen hashed brown potatoes
1 package (10 ounces) frozen chopped spinach
1 tablespoon minced onion
1/2 teaspoon lemon pepper
1/2 cup Cheese Sauce (variation, White Sauce, page 73)
4 eggs
1 tablespoon butter or margarine
1/4 cup dry bread crumbs

Use DEFROST cycle and cook potatoes and spinach 12 to 15 minutes, or until thawed. Drain spinach well. In 1 1/2-quart oval or round shallow microproof dish, combine potato, spinach, onion, and pepper; set aside. Prepare Cheese Sauce and pour over spinach. Make 4 indentations in spinach mixture; break 1 egg into each. Pierce each yolk. Set aside. Place butter in small microproof dish. Use COOK cycle and cook 30 seconds. Stir in bread crumbs. Sprinkle over eggs. Cover with waxed paper. Use COOK cycle and cook 9 to 11 minutes, or until eggs are almost set. Let stand 3 minutes before serving.

Low-Cal Eggs Oriental ———————— 2 to 3 servings
Total Cooking Time: 9 to 9½ minutes

1 tablespoon butter or
  margarine
½ cup sliced mushrooms
1 cup chopped green onions
4 eggs
4 tablespoons water
1 can (8 ounces) sliced
  water chestnuts
1 cup alfalfa sprouts
½ teaspoon salt
¼ teaspoon freshly ground
  pepper

Place butter in 8-inch microproof pie plate. Use COOK cycle and cook 30 seconds, or until melted. Add mushrooms and onions. Cover with waxed paper. Use COOK cycle and cook 3 minutes. In small bowl, mix remaining ingredients. Add to onions and mushrooms; stir lightly to mix. Cover. Use COOK cycle and cook 5½ to 6 minutes, or until eggs are set, stirring every 2 minutes during cooking time. Let stand 1 to 2 minutes. Sprinkle with additional sprouts. Serve with soy sauce, if desired.

Classic Omelet ————————————— 2 servings
Total Cooking Time: 4½ to 5 minutes

1 tablespoon butter or
  margarine
4 eggs
4 tablespoons water
½ teaspoon salt
⅛ teaspoon freshly ground
  pepper

Place butter in 9-inch microproof pie plate. Use COOK cycle and cook 30 seconds, or until melted. Beat remaining ingredients in bowl; pour into pie plate. Cover with waxed paper. Use COOK cycle and cook 4 to 4½ minutes, stirring once during cooking time. Let stand, covered, 1 to 2 minutes. Fold in half to serve.

Spanish Omelet ——————————— 4 servings

Total Cooking Time: 13½ to 14 minutes

1 tablespoon butter or
    margarine
½ cup chopped onion
⅓ cup chopped green pepper
1 cup tomato sauce or
    tomatoes with bits
½ teaspoon salt
¼ to ½ teaspoon
    hot pepper sauce
2 Classic Omelets (page 79)

In 4-cup glass measure, combine butter, onion, and green pepper. Use COOK cycle and cook 4 minutes, or until onion is transparent. Add remaining ingredients, except omelets. Use COOK cycle and cook 5 minutes, or until mixture boils.

Prepare Classic Omelets. Before folding in half, spoon one-fourth of the tomato mixture on each omelet. Serve topped with remaining mixture.

Jelly Omelet ——————————— 2 servings

Total Cooking Time: 4½ to 5 minutes

1 tablespoon butter or
    margarine
4 eggs
4 tablespoons water
½ teaspoon salt
⅛ teaspoon freshly ground
    pepper
⅓ cup currant or other
    tart jelly

Place butter in 9-inch microproof pie plate. Use COOK cycle and cook 30 seconds, or until melted. In small bowl, beat remaining ingredients, except jelly, with fork. Pour into pie plate. Cover with waxed paper. Use COOK cycle and cook 3 minutes, stirring once during cooking time. Cover. Use COOK cycle and cook 1 to 1½ minutes; stir. Let stand, covered, 1 to 2 minutes. Spread jelly over bottom half of omelet; fold top half over jelly. Cut in half. Serve hot.

←*Spanish Omelet*

Fiesta Pie ——————————— 2 to 3 servings
Total Cooking Time: 5½ to 6 minutes

1 tablespoon butter or margarine
4 eggs
4 tablespoons water
2 tablespoons chopped mild green chilies
1½ teaspoons onion flakes
½ teaspoon chili powder
½ teaspoon salt
¼ teaspoon freshly ground pepper
½ cup shredded sharp Cheddar cheese
1 medium tomato, cut in wedges

Place butter in 8-inch microproof pie plate. Use COOK cycle and cook 30 seconds, or until melted. In small bowl, combine remaining ingredients, except cheese and tomato. Pour into pie plate. Cover with waxed paper. Use COOK cycle and cook 3 minutes. Stir lightly; use COOK cycle and cook 2 to 2½ minutes, or until eggs are almost set in center. Sprinkle with cheese. Let stand, covered, 5 minutes, or until cheese is melted. Serve garnished with tomato wedges.

Cheese Fondue ——————————— 4 to 6 servings
Total Cooking Time: 9 to 11 minutes

1 pound (4 cups) shredded Swiss cheese
2 tablespoons cornstarch
1½ cups dry white wine
1 small clove garlic, minced
Dash salt
Freshly ground pepper
French bread, cut in cubes
Assorted vegetables

Combine cheese and cornstarch in 2-quart microproof casserole. Stir in wine, garlic, salt and pepper. Use COOK cycle and cook 9 to 11 minutes, or until cheese is melted and smooth, stirring twice during cooking time. Pour into fondue pot and keep warm. If mixture becomes too thick, add more wine. Serve with bread cubes and assorted vegetables.

This recipe can be doubled. Use COOK cycle and cook 12 to 15 minutes.

ONE-DISH DINNERS

Some casseroles need occasional stirring. Use hot pads when the dish is hot (left). Large items, such as chicken pieces, are rearranged using tongs (above).

By now, we think you should have a pretty good notion about the speed of microwave cooking. But let's not forget those time-saving and tasty casseroles, perhaps the first cooking shortcuts in conventional cooking. No doubt the first "casserole" was developed over an open fire!

It probably won't surprise you either to learn that the microwave oven is specially suited to casserole cooking. Convenience plus speed make those one-dish wonders better than ever.

Because no heat is applied to the casserole dish, food does not stick. And, of course, you can do ingredient preparation, such as sautéing onions or precooking meat, right in the same dish in the microwave oven. No stovetop steps at all!

We've assembled a balanced collection of some traditional casseroles plus a few unique ideas. We hope you will want to try all of them.

Converting Your Recipes

It's so easy to convert your own casserole recipes that you'll probably need to adjust only three items, if at all. They are: a reduction in the amount of liquid because little evaporation occurs in the microwave oven; changing from long-grain rice or dried beans to quick-cooking or precooked, canned types; and, doing some steps first, such as cooking onion to be sure it is tender. For more help, read the casserole information on page 30 and these tips:

☐ Most ground beef casseroles call for extra lean meat. If you are using regular ground beef, partially cook and then drain fat before adding other ingredients.
☐ Many casserole dishes have their own lids. However, often those lids, especially decorative ones, make large casseroles too tall for the oven. When necessary, cover with plastic wrap instead.
☐ With the microwave oven, casseroles can go right from the freezer to the oven for defrosting and cooking. For a 2-quart casserole, use DEFROST cycle and cook for 15 to 18 minutes. Let stand, covered, for 5 minutes. Stir. Use COOK cycle and cook 12 to 15 minutes, stirring twice during cooking.
☐ Special microwave meat thermometers are useful when you want to determine precise casserole temperatures. 150°F is the recommended temperature.

Bavarian Wiener Supper ——————— 5 to 6 servings
Total Cooking Time: 13 to 15 minutes

1 pound (about 10) frankfurters
1 can (10¾ ounces) condensed cream of mushroom soup
½ cup mayonnaise
1 can (14 ounces) sauerkraut, drained
1 teaspoon caraway seed
4 cups diced cooked potatoes
½ cup buttered bread crumbs
¼ teaspoon paprika

Cut 3 of the frankfurters in half lengthwise; set aside. Slice remaining frankfurters ¼ inch thick. In small bowl, combine soup and mayonnaise; set aside. In shallow 2-quart microproof casserole, combine sauerkraut, caraway, sliced frankfurters, and half of soup mixture; spread evenly. In separate bowl, mix remaining soup mixture with potatoes; spoon around edges of dish. Sprinkle bread crumbs over potatoes. Sprinkle with paprika. Arrange halved frankfurters decoratively in center. Use COOK cycle and cook 13 to 15 minutes, or until heated through. Let stand 3 minutes before serving.

Ground Beef Gumbo ———————— 4 to 5 servings
Total Cooking Time: 15 minutes

1 pound lean ground beef
¼ cup chopped onion
2 tablespoons chopped green pepper
1 can (10¾ ounces) chicken gumbo soup
¼ teaspoon salt
⅛ teaspoon freshly ground pepper
2 cups hot cooked rice

·Combine beef, onion, and green pepper in 2-quart microproof casserole. Use COOK cycle and cook 10 minutes, or until beef is no longer red, stirring once during cooking. Break up beef with fork; drain. Stir in remaining ingredients, except rice. Cover. Use COOK cycle and cook 5 minutes, stirring once during cooking time. Serve over rice.

Ground Beef Gumbo can also be served as a sandwich filling in hamburger buns.

Cowboy Beef Casserole ———————— 5 to 6 servings
Total Cooking Time: 19 to 21 minutes

1 pound lean ground beef
¼ cup chopped onion
¼ cup chopped green pepper
1 can (16 ounces) tomatoes, drained and diced, liquid reserved
1 can (12 ounces) whole kernel corn, drained
1 can (8 ounces) tomato sauce
½ cup sliced stuffed olives
1 to 2 teaspoons chili powder
1 cup coarsely crushed corn chips
½ cup shredded Cheddar cheese

Place beef in 2-quart microproof casserole; break up with fork. Add onion and green pepper. Use COOK cycle and cook 10 minutes, or until beef is no longer red; drain. Stir to break up beef. Add tomatoes to meat mixture. Stir in ¼ cup reserved tomato liquid, corn, tomato sauce, olives, and chili powder. Cover. Use COOK cycle and cook 7 to 9 minutes, or until heated through; stir. Sprinkle with corn chips and cheese. Use DEFROST cycle and cook 2 minutes, or until cheese is melted. Let stand 3 minutes before serving.

Italian Beef Casserole —————— 6 to 8 servings
Total Cooking Time: 30 to 32 minutes

1 pound lean ground beef
1 can (15½ ounces)
  spaghetti sauce
1¼ cups water
1 can (16 ounces) cut green
  beans, drained
1 package (7 ounces) elbow
  macaroni
2 tablespoons dry onion
  flakes
1 tablespoon sugar
1 tablespoon Italian
  seasoning
½ teaspoon garlic powder
½ teaspoon salt
⅛ teaspoon freshly ground
  pepper
1 cup shredded mozzarella
  cheese

Place ground beef in 3-quart microproof casserole; break up with fork. Use COOK cycle and cook 6 to 8 minutes, or until beef is no longer red. Break up any large pieces; drain. Add remaining ingredients, except cheese; mix well. Cover. Use COOK cycle and cook 10 minutes. Stir; cover. Use COOK cycle and cook 14 minutes. Sprinkle with cheese. Cover and let stand 10 minutes before serving.

Beefburger Stroganoff —————— 6 servings
Total Cooking Time: 24 to 26 minutes

1 pound lean ground beef
1 small onion, chopped
1 clove garlic, minced
1 can (10¾ ounces)
  condensed cream of
  chicken soup
1 can (8 ounces) mushroom
  stems and pieces,
  drained
2 tablespoons tomato paste
¼ teaspoon salt
⅛ teaspoon freshly ground
  pepper
1 cup dairy sour cream
2 tablespoons chopped
  fresh parsley
4 cups hot cooked rice
  or noodles

Place ground beef in 2-quart microproof casserole; break up with fork. Stir in onion and garlic. Use COOK cycle and cook 10 to 12 minutes, or until beef is no longer red and onion is transparent; drain. Stir in soup, mushrooms, tomato paste, salt, and pepper. Cover. Use COOK cycle and cook 12 minutes, stirring once. Stir in sour cream. Use DEFROST cycle and cook 2 minutes; stir. Sprinkle with parsley. Serve over rice or noodles.

Garlic Bread (page 159), Italian Beef Casserole→

Chili Beef and Chips ——————— 6 to 8 servings

Total Cooking Time: 27 to 29 minutes

1 pound lean ground beef
½ cup chopped onion
1 clove garlic, minced
1 can (10¾ ounces) condensed cream of mushroom soup
1 can (4 ounces) chopped green chilies
1 can (10 ounces) mild enchilada sauce
1 package (6¼ ounces) corn or tortilla chips
2 cups shredded Cheddar cheese
2 tablespoons chopped black olives

Place ground beef in 2-quart glass measure or microproof casserole; break up with fork. Add onion and garlic. Use COOK cycle and cook 10 minutes, or until beef is no longer red and onion is transparent. Stir to break up meat; drain. Stir in soup and chilies. In 10×8×2-inch oval microproof casserole, place about 2 cups corn chips. Layer half each of the meat mixture, enchilada sauce, and cheese. Repeat. Use COOK cycle and cook 17 to 19 minutes, or until heated through. Sprinkle with remaining corn chips and olives. Let stand 3 minutes before serving.

Stuffed Cabbage Roll Casserole —————————— 8 servings

Total Cooking Time: 33 to 37 minutes

8 large cabbage leaves (use outer leaves)
½ cup water
1 pound lean ground beef
3 tablespoons chopped onion
1 cup quick-cooking rice
1 egg, slightly beaten
1 teaspoon salt
⅛ teaspoon freshly ground pepper
1½ cups tomato juice
1 can (10½ ounces) pizza sauce
1 teaspoon sugar
½ teaspoon oregano

Place cabbage leaves and water in 3-quart microproof casserole. Cover. Use COOK cycle and cook 9 to 11 minutes, or until leaves are pliable. Place ground beef in 4-cup glass measure; break up with fork. Stir in onion. Use COOK cycle and cook 6 minutes, or until beef is partially cooked and onion is transparent; drain and cool. Stir in rice, egg, salt, and pepper. Drain cabbage. Divide beef mixture (about ⅓ cup) among cabbage leaves, spooning onto center of each. Roll up; secure with toothpick, if necessary. Place cabbage rolls in 3-quart casserole, seam-side down.

In small bowl, blend tomato juice, pizza sauce, sugar, and oregano. Pour over cabbage rolls; cover. Use COOK cycle and cook 18 to 20 minutes, or until tender, rearranging cabbage rolls and basting with sauce after 10 minutes.

Supper Pie ———————————————— 6 servings
Total Cooking Time: 23½ to 25½ minutes

1 package (8 ounces)
  spaghetti, cooked
1 egg, slightly beaten
⅓ cup grated Parmesan
  cheese
1 tablespoon butter or
  margarine
1 tablespoon parsley flakes
¾ pound lean ground beef
1 onion, finely chopped
1 clove garlic, minced
1 can (8 ounces) whole
  tomatoes, drained
  and cut in pieces,
  liquid reserved
1 can (6 ounces) tomato
  paste
½ teaspoon oregano
½ teaspoon salt
¼ teaspoon freshly ground
  pepper
1 cup ricotta cheese
½ cup shredded Monterey
  Jack or mozzarella
  cheese

In large bowl, combine spaghetti, egg, butter, Parmesan cheese, and parsley; stir until butter is melted. Turn into 10-inch microproof pie plate; press mixture evenly onto bottom and sides. Use COOK cycle and cook 2½ minutes, rotating after 1 minute; set aside.

Combine ground beef, onion, and garlic in 2-quart microproof bowl; break up beef with fork. Use COOK cycle and cook 9 to 10 minutes, or until beef is no longer red; drain. Add tomatoes, tomato paste, oregano, salt, and pepper. Use COOK cycle and cook 5 minutes.

Spread ricotta cheese over spaghetti; pour meat mixture over ricotta cheese. Cover with waxed paper. Use COOK cycle and cook 7 to 8 minutes, or until heated through. Sprinkle with shredded cheese. Cover and let stand 3 minutes until cheese is melted. Serve hot.

Macaroni and Cheese ——————— 4 to 6 servings
Total Cooking Time: 11 to 13 minutes

2 cups elbow macaroni
2 tablespoons butter or
  margarine
2 tablespoons flour
2 cups milk
1 teaspoon salt
1 tablespoon instant minced
  onion
2 cups shredded Cheddar
  cheese

Cook macaroni according to package directions; drain. Place in 2-quart microproof casserole; set aside. Place butter in 4-cup measure. Use COOK cycle and cook 1 minute, or until melted. Stir in flour until blended.

Pour milk into 2-cup glass measure. Use COOK cycle and cook 3 minutes. Stir into flour-butter mixture. Use COOK cycle and cook 7 to 9 minutes, or until thickened, stirring frequently. Add salt and onion. Add cheese; stir until melted. Pour over macaroni; blend well. Serve immediately.

Ham, Asparagus, and
Noodle Casserole _____ 6 servings

Total Cooking Time: 12 to 15 minutes

2 cups cooked noodles
1 tablespoon parsley flakes
1 cup milk
2 tablespoons butter or margarine
2 tablespoons all-purpose flour
½ teaspoon salt
¼ teaspoon white pepper
1 package (3 ounces) cream cheese, cut up
6 slices boiled ham
3 teaspoons prepared mustard
1 can (14½ ounces) asparagus spears or 18 fresh asparagus spears, cooked and drained
Paprika

Combine noodles with parsley; mix lightly; set aside.

Pour milk into 2-cup glass measure. Use COOK cycle and cook 2 minutes, or until heated through; set aside. Place butter in another 2-cup glass measure. Use COOK cycle and cook 1 minute. Stir in flour; blend well. Use COOK cycle and cook 1 minute. Briskly stir in warm milk, salt, and pepper. Use COOK cycle and cook 3 to 4 minutes, or until boiling and thickened, stirring once during cooking. Stir in cream cheese until melted.

Pour half of sauce over noodles; stir to coat. Spread noodle mixture in shallow 1½-quart round or oval microproof dish.

Spread ½ teaspoon mustard on each ham slice. Roll up 3 asparagus spears in each ham slice. Place ham rolls, seam side down, over noodles. Pour remaining sauce over ham. Sprinkle with paprika. Use COOK cycle and cook 5 to 7 minutes, or until heated through. Let stand 2 minutes before serving.

Chicken and Rice Casserole _____ 4 to 6 servings

Total Cooking Time: 20 to 22 minutes

2 cups boned chicken, cut in 1-inch cubes
1 can (10¾ ounces) condensed cream of chicken soup
1 cup milk
1 cup sliced mushrooms
⅔ cup quick-cooking rice
1 envelope dry onion soup mix
¼ teaspoon poultry seasoning
½ cup shredded Cheddar cheese

Combine all ingredients, except cheese, in 1½-quart microproof casserole. Cover with plastic wrap. Use COOK cycle and cook 20 to 22 minutes, stirring twice during cooking time. Sprinkle with cheese. Cover and let stand 10 minutes before serving.

←*Ham, Asparagus, and Noodle Casserole*

Cantonese Beef and Vegetables ─────────── 4 to 5 servings
Total Cooking Time: 16 to 19 minutes

¼ cup dry sherry
¼ cup soy sauce
¼ cup water
1 tablespoon sugar
1 clove garlic, minced
1 pound boneless beef steak,
   such as sirloin,
   thinly sliced
6 green onions
1 small head cauliflower
1 package (7 ounces) frozen
   pea pods
1 can (5 ounces) sliced
   water chestnuts,
   drained

In 2-quart microproof dish, combine sherry, soy sauce, water, sugar, and garlic. Add beef; stir. Cover with plastic wrap. Let stand, at room temperature, 4 hours, stirring occasionally.
   Cut onions, white and green part, in 2-inch pieces; split lengthwise; set aside. Separate cauliflower into florets; slice each ¼-inch thick; set aside. Stir onions and cauliflower into beef mixture. Cover. Use COOK cycle and cook 13 to 15 minutes, stirring once during cooking time. Stir in frozen pea pods and water chestnuts. Cover. Use COOK cycle and cook 3 to 4 minutes, or until pea pods and cauliflower are crisp-tender. Serve over hot cooked rice.

Hearty Beef Vegetable Stew ─────────── 6 to 8 servings
Total Cooking Time: 30 to 32 minutes

2¼ cups water, divided
2 beef bouillon cubes
1 pound round steak, cut
   in ½-inch cubes
3 tablespoons cornstarch
2 large potatoes, peeled
   and cubed
¾ cup thinly sliced carrots
½ cup thinly sliced celery
1 medium onion, diced
½ teaspoon salt
¼ teaspoon freshly ground
   pepper
¼ teaspoon thyme
1 bay leaf, crushed

Combine 2 cups of the water, bouillon cubes, and beef in 2-quart microproof bowl. Use COOK cycle and cook 20 minutes, or until steak is tender. In 1-cup microproof measure, mix remaining ¼ cup water and cornstarch. Add cornstarch and remaining ingredients to beef; stir. Cover with waxed paper. Use COOK cycle and cook 10 to 12 minutes, or until vegetables are tender. Cover and let stand 10 minutes before serving.

Ham and Potato Scallop _____ 4 servings
Total Cooking Time: 24 to 26 minutes

1 cup milk
2 tablespoons butter or margarine
2 tablespoons all-purpose flour
1 teaspoon prepared mustard
1/2 teaspoon salt
1/4 teaspoon white pepper
3 medium potatoes, peeled and thinly sliced (about 1 1/2 cups)
1 1/2 cups cooked diced ham
1 teaspoon minced onion
1/4 cup shredded Cheddar cheese

Pour milk into 2-cup glass measure. Use COOK cycle and cook 2 minutes; set aside. Place butter in 2-cup glass measure. Use COOK cycle and cook 1 minute. Stir in flour. Use COOK cycle and cook 1 minute. Briskly stir hot milk, prepared mustard, salt, and pepper into butter. Set aside. Place potatoes in 1 1/2-quart microproof casserole. Add ham and onion. Pour white sauce over ham and potatoes mixture; sitr to combine. Cover with waxed paper. Use COOK cycle and cook 20 to 22 minutes, stirring twice during cooking time. Sprinkle with cheese. Cover and let stand 10 minutes, or until cheese is melted.

Chicken and Spinach Casserole _____ 4 servings
Total Cooking Time: 27 to 30 minutes

4 tablespoons butter or margarine, divided
1/2 cup chopped onion
2 packages (10 ounces each) frozen chopped spinach, thawed and thoroughly drained
2 cups diced cooked chicken
1 can (10 3/4 ounces) condensed cream of chicken soup
1 cup shredded Swiss cheese
3 tablespoons chicken broth
2/3 cup bread crumbs
Paprika

In 1-cup glass measure, combine 1 tablespoon butter with onion. Use COOK cycle and cook 4 to 5 minutes, or until onion is tender. Stir onion into spinach. Spread mixture in 9-inch pie plate. Spoon chicken evenly over spinach. Set aside. Combine soup, cheese, and broth in 4-cup glass measure. Use COOK cycle and cook 6 minutes; stir to melt cheese. Pour evenly over chicken. Combine bread crumbs and remaining 3 tablespoons butter in 2-cup glass measure. Use COOK cycle and cook 2 minutes; stir to blend. Sprinkle bread crumbs on top. Sprinkle with paprika. Use COOK cycle and cook 15 to 17 minutes.

Stir-Fry Shrimp and Vegetables _____ 4 servings

Total Cooking Time: 8 to 9 minutes

1 tablespoon cornstarch
3/4 cup water
2 tablespoons soy sauce
1/4 teaspoon bead molasses
2 cups broccoli florets
1 can (4 1/4 ounces) large
   shrimp, drained
1 small onion, diced
2 cups hot cooked rice

Mix together cornstarch, water, soy sauce, and molasses; set aside. Combine broccoli, shrimp, and onions in 1-quart microproof casserole; add sauce mixture. Use COOK cycle and cook 6 minutes, stirring halfway through cooking time. Stir; cover with waxed paper. Use COOK cycle and cook 2 to 3 minutes, or until broccoli is crisp-tender. Cover and let stand 5 minutes before serving. Serve over rice.

Tuna-Cashew Casserole _____ 5 to 6 servings

Total Cooking Time: 12 to 14 minutes

1 can (10 3/4 ounces)
   condensed cream of
   mushroom soup
3/4 cup milk
3 cups cooked noodles
1 can (6 1/2 ounces) tuna,
   drained and flaked
1/2 cup diced celery
1/2 cup broken salted cashew
   nuts
1 tablespoon instant minced
   onion
1/2 teaspoon salt
1/8 teaspoon freshly ground
   pepper
1/4 cup crushed soda crackers

Blend soup and milk in 2-quart microproof casserole. Add remaining ingredients, except crackers; blend well. Use COOK cycle and cook 9 minutes; stir. Top with cracker crumbs. Use COOK cycle and cook 3 to 5 minutes, or until hot in center.

BUDGET-WISE MEAT

Arrangement is important when cooking meat (left). A microwave food thermometer is helpful in determining preferred doneness for meat (above).

Cooking meat in the microwave oven offers tremendous advantages. For best results, one should follow a recipe designed for microwave cooking. Since the meat cooks so rapidly, care must be taken to avoid overcooking tender cuts of meat. Pot roasts and less tender cuts which require long, moist cooking for the connective tissue to break down, need only the proper understanding for succulent results — with much less cooking time than conventional methods. Trimming the fat to allow the microwave energy to reach the meat itself is an important technique to follow. Also, the use of a browning agent, such as paprika, soy sauce, onion soup mix, tomato sauce, or a flavoring that enhances the recipe as well as giving it a rich color, is part of learning how to cook the microwave way.

Try our attractive Polynesian Pork Kabobs (page 108), Super Meatloaf Ring (page 104), or Pot Roast and Vegetables (page 106).

Converting Your Recipes

Charts on the following pages outline microwave thawing and cooking times for the standard cuts of meat. For converting meatloaf, meat in sauces, and recipes that call for less tender cuts of meat, you're sure to find a similar recipe here to guide your own creations. Adapt your conventional recipes by matching ingredients and methods as closely as possible. Experiment as much as you like. Here are some helpful hints:

If you don't have a microproof ring mold, you can make one easily. Insert a small straight-sided glass, open end up, in the center of a glass or ceramic round baking dish.

☐ Recipe times here presume meat is at refrigerator temperature. If your meal requires lengthy preparation, during which the meat may reach room temperature, reduce cooking times.

☐ Baste, marinate, or season meat just as you would for conventional cooking.

☐ You can use a microwave roasting rack to elevate meat from its drippings during cooking, if you so desire.

☐ Check dishes that use relatively long cooking times to be sure liquid has not evaporated. Add liquid as necessary.

The Defrosting Guide

1. You may begin defrosting meat within its original paper or plastic wrappings. However, meat will defrost more evenly if removed from its original wrapping as soon as possible. Remove all metal rings, wire twist ties, and all foil wrapping.

2. Place meat in microproof dish.

3. Defrost in the microwave oven only as long as necessary, since standing time will complete the thawing process.

4. Slightly increase the time for weights larger than on the chart. Do not double.

DEFROSTING GUIDE — MEAT

Meat	Amount	Control	Time (minutes per pound)	Standing Time (minutes)	Special Notes
Beef					
Ground beef	1-lb.	DEFROST	5 - 6	5	Turn over once. Remove
	2-lbs.	DEFROST	8 - 9	5	thawed portions with fork. Return remainder. Freeze in doughnut shape.
	¼-lb. patty	DEFROST	1 per patty	2	Depress center when freezing. Defrost on plate.
Pot roast, chuck	under 4 lbs.	DEFROST	3 - 5	10	Turn over once.
	over 4 lbs.	COOK	3 - 6	10	Turn over once.
Rib roast, rolled	3 to 4 lbs.	DEFROST	6 - 8	30 - 45	Turn over once.
	6 to 8 lbs.	COOK	7 - 9	90	Turn over twice.
Rib roast, bone in		COOK	6 - 7	45 - 90	Turn over twice.
Rump roast	3 to 4 lbs.	DEFROST	3 - 5	30	Turn over once.
	6 to 7 lbs.	COOK	3 - 6	45	Turn over twice.
Round steak		DEFROST	4 - 5	5 - 10	Turn over once.
Flank steak		DEFROST	4 - 5	5 - 10	Turn over once.
Sirloin steak	1/2″ thick	DEFROST	4 - 5	5 - 10	Turn over once.
Tenderloin, whole	2 to 3 lbs.	DEFROST	5 - 6	10	Turn over once.
steak	12 oz.	DEFROST	3 - 4	8 - 10	Turn over once.
Stew beef	2 lbs.	DEFROST	3 - 5	8 - 10	Turn over once. Separate.
Lamb					
Cubed for stew		DEFROST	7 - 8	5	Turn over once. Separate.
Ground lamb	under 4 lbs.	DEFROST	3 - 5	30 - 45	Turn over once.
	over 4 lbs.	COOK	3 - 6	30 - 45	Turn over twice.
Chops	1″ thick	DEFROST	5 - 8	15	Turn over twice.
Leg	5 - 8 lbs.	DEFROST	4 - 5	15 - 20	Turn over twice.
Pork					
Chops	1/2″	DEFROST	4 - 6	5 - 10	Separate chops halfway
	1″	DEFROST	5 - 7	10	through defrosting time.
Spareribs, country-style ribs		DEFROST	5 - 7	10	Turn over once.
Roast	under 4 lbs.	DEFROST	4 - 5	30 - 45	Turn over once.
	over 4 lbs.	COOK	5 - 6	30 - 45	Turn over twice.
Bacon	1-lb.	DEFROST	2 - 3	3 - 5	Defrost until strips separate.
Sausage, bulk	1 lb.	DEFROST	2 - 3	3 - 5	Turn over once. Remove thawed portions with fork. Return remainder.
Sausage links	1 lb.	DEFROST	3 - 5	4 - 6	Turn over once. Defrost until pieces can be separated.
Hot dogs		DEFROST	5 - 6	5	
Veal					
Roast	3 to 4 lbs.	DEFROST	5 - 7	30	Turn over once.
	6 to 7 lbs.	COOK	6 - 8	90	Turn over twice.
Chops	1/2″ thick	DEFROST	4 - 6	20	Turn over once. Separate chops and continue defrosting.
Variety Meat					
Liver		DEFROST	5 - 6	10	Turn over once.
Tongue		DEFROST	7 - 8	10	Turn over once.

Using the Cooking Guide

1. Meat should be completely thawed before cooking.
2. Place meat, fat side down, on microwave roasting rack set in glass baking dish. An inverted microproof saucer may be used if you do not have a roasting rack.
3. Meat may be covered lightly with waxed paper to stop splatters.
4. Use a microwave meat thermometer for the most accurate cooking of larger meat cuts.

5. Unless otherwise noted, times given for steaks and patties will give medium doneness.
6. During standing time, the internal temperature of roasts will rise approximately 15°F. Hence, standing time is considered an essential part of the time required to complete cooking.
7. Cutlets and chops that are breaded are cooked in the same time as shown on chart.

COOKING GUIDE — MEAT
Use COOK cycle.

Meat	Amount	First Cook Time	Second Cook Time	Standing Time (minutes)	Special Notes
Beef					
Ground beef	Bulk	3 minutes per pound	Stir. 3 minutes per pound	5	Crumble in dish, cook covered.
Ground beef patties, 4 oz., 1/2" thick	1	1½ - 2 minutes	Turn over. 1½ - 2 minutes		Shallow baking dish.
	2	2½ - 3 minutes	Turn over. 2½ - 3 minutes		Shallow baking dish.
	4	4½ minutes	Turn over. 4½ - 5 minutes		Shallow baking dish.
Meatloaf	2 lbs.	16 - 20 minutes		5 - 10	Glass loaf dish or glass ring mold.
Beef rib roast, boneless		Rare: 5½ - 6 minutes per pound Medium: 6½ - 8 minutes per pound Well: 8 - 9½ minutes per pound	Turn over. 4 - 5 minutes per pound 6 - 6½ minutes per pound 7 - 8 minutes per pound	10 10 10	Glass baking dish with microproof roasting rack.
Rib roast, bone in		Rare: 4 - 5½ minutes per pound Medium: 5½ - 6½ minutes per pound Well: 6½ - 8 minutes per pound	Turn over. 4 - 5 minutes per pound 4 - 6 minutes per pound 6 - 7 minutes per pound	10	Glass baking dish with microproof roasting rack.

Meat	Amount	First Cook Time	Second Cook Time	Standing Time (minutes)	Special Notes
Beef round, rump, or chuck, boneless		6½ minutes per pound	Turn over. 19 minutes per pound	10 - 15	Casserole with tight cover. Requires liquid.
Beef brisket, boneless, fresh or corned	2 - 3 lbs.	6½ minutes per pound	Turn over. 19 minutes per pound	10 - 15	3-quart casserole Dutch oven with tight cover. Water to cover.
Top round steak		6½ minutes per pound	Turn over. 5 minutes per pound	10 - 15	Casserole with tight cover. Requires liquid.
Sirloin steak	¾ to 1" thick	6½ minutes per pound	Drain dish and turn over. 2½ minutes per pound	10 - 15	Shallow cooking dish or browning dish preheated 11 minutes on COOK.
Minute steak or cube steak	4, 6-oz. steaks	1½ - 2½ minutes	Drain dish and turn over. 1½ - 2½ minutes		Browning dish preheated on COOK 11 minutes.
Tenderloin	4, 8-oz. steaks	Rare: 6½ minutes Med: 8 minutes Well: 12 minutes	Drain, turn steak. 1½ - 2½ minutes 2½ - 4 minutes 2½ - 4 minutes	10 - 15	Browning dish preheated on COOK 11 minutes.
Rib eye or strip steak	1½ - 2 lbs.	Rare: 5½ minutes Med: 6½ minutes Well: 9½ minutes	Drain, turn steak. 1 - 1½ minutes 1½ - 2½ minutes 2½ - 4 minutes	10 - 15	Browning dish preheated on COOK 11 minutes.
Lamb					
Ground lamb patties	1 - 2 lbs.	5 minutes	Turn over. 5½ - 6½ minutes		Browning dish preheated on COOK 10 minutes.
Lamb chops	1 - 1½ lbs. 1" thick	10½ minutes	Turn over. 9½ - 10½ minutes		Browning dish preheated on COOK 10 minutes.
Lamb leg or shoulder roast, bone in		Medium: 4 - 5 minutes per pound Well: 5 - 6 minutes per pound	Cover end of leg bone with foil. Turn over. Medium: 4 - 5 minutes per pound Well: 5 - 6 minutes per pound	5 10	6 × 9-inch dish with microproof roasting rack.
Lamb roast, boneless		6 - 7 minutes per pound	Turn over. 6 - 7 minutes per pound	10	6 × 9-inch dish with microproof roasting rack.
Veal					
Shoulder or rump roast, boneless	2 - 4 lbs.	9 minutes per pound	Turn over. 10 - 12 minutes per pound	10	6 × 9-inch dish with microproof roasting rack.
Veal cutlets or loin chops	1/2" thick	2½ minutes per pound	Turn over. 2½ - 5½ minutes per pound		Browning dish preheated on COOK 10 - 12 minutes.
Pork					
Pork chops	1/2" thick	8 minutes per pound	Turn over. 6½ - 8 minutes per pound		Browning dish preheated on COOK 10 minutes.
Spareribs		7 - 8 minutes per pound	Turn over. 7 - 8 minutes per pound	10	6 × 9-inch dish with microproof roasting rack.

Meat	Amount	First Cook Time	Second Cook Time	Standing Time (minutes)	Special Notes
Pork loin roast, boneless	3 - 5 lbs.	8 minutes per pound	Turn over. 6 - 7 minutes per pound	10	6 × 9-inch dish with microproof roasting rack.
Pork loin, center cut	4 - 5 lbs.	6½ - 8 minutes per pound	Turn over. 4 - 6 minutes per pound	10	6 × 9-inch dish with microproof roasting rack.
Ham, boneless, precooked		6 - 8 minutes per pound	Turn over. 6 - 8 minutes per pound	10	6 × 9-inch dish with microproof roasting rack.
Center cut ham slice	1 - 1½ lbs.	6 minutes per pound	Turn over. 6 - 7 minutes per pound	10	6 × 9-inch baking dish.
Smoked ham shank		4 - 6 minutes per pound	Turn over. 4 - 6 minutes per pound	10	6 × 9-inch dish with microproof roasting rack.
Canned ham	3 lbs.	6 - 7 minutes per pound	6 - 7 minutes per pound	10	6 × 9-inch dish with microproof roasting rack.
	5 lbs.	4 - 6 minutes per pound	Turn over. 4 - 6 minutes per pound	10	6 × 9-inch dish with microproof roasting rack.
Sausage patties	12-oz.	2½ minutes	Turn over. 2 - 2½ minutes per pound		Browning dish preheated on COOK 10 minutes.
Sausage	16 oz.	4 minutes	Stir. 1½ - 2½ minutes		Crumble into 1½-quart dish, covered.
Pork sausage links	½ lb. 1 lb.	Pierce casing. 1½ minutes 2½ - 3 minutes	Turn over. 1½ - 2 minutes 2½ - 3 minutes		Browning dish preheated on COOK 10 minutes.
Bratwurst, precooked		Pierce casing. 6 minutes per pound	Rearrange. 5 - 6 minutes per pound		Casserole.
Polish sausage, knockwurst, ring bologna		Pierce casing. 2½ - 3½ minutes per pound	Rearrange. 2½ - 3½ minutes per pound		Casserole.
Hot dogs	1 2 4	30 - 45 seconds 50 - 60 seconds 1 - 1½ minutes			Shallow dish. Shallow dish. Shallow dish.
Bacon	2 slices	2½ - 3 minutes			Dish; slices between paper towels.
	4 slices	4½ - 5 minutes			Dish; slices between paper towels.
	6 slices	6½ - 7 minutes			Roasting rack, slices covered with paper towels.
	8 slices	8 - 10 minutes			Roasting rack, slices covered with paper towels.

Special Tips about Bacon

☐ Cook bacon on paper-lined plate, and cover with paper towels to prevent splatters and absorb drippings.

☐ To reserve drippings, cook bacon on a meat rack in a baking dish or on a microwave bacon rack. Bacon can also be cooked, in slices or cut up, in a casserole and removed if necessary with a slotted spoon.

☐ For bacon that is soft rather than crisp, cook at the minimum timing.

☐ Bacon varies in quality. The thickness and amount of sugar and salt used in curing will affect browning and timing. Cook thicker slices a bit longer than the chart indicates. You will also find that sweeter bacon cooks more quickly.

☐ Sugar in bacon causes brown spots to appear on the paper towels. If the bacon tends to stick a bit to the towel, it is due to an extra high amount of sugar.

COOKING/DEFROSTING GUIDE — CONVENIENCE BEEF

Food	Amount	Control	Time (minutes)	Special Notes
Barbecued beef, chili, stew, hash, meatballs, etc.	16 oz. or less (cans)	COOK	3½ - 5½	Remove from cans to microproof plate or casserole, cover. Stir halfway through cooking time.
Stuffed peppers, cabbage rolls, chow mein, etc.	16 - 32 oz. (cans)	COOK	5 - 9	
Barbecued beef, chili, stew, corned beef hash, meatballs, patties in sauce, gravy	8 - 16 oz. package (frozen)	COOK	6½ - 14	Remove from foil container to microproof casserole, cover. Slit plastic pouches.
Dry casserole mixes, cooked hamburger added	6½ - 8 oz. package	COOK	24 - 30	Remove mix from package to 3-quart microproof casserole. Cover. Stir once.

Porcupine Meatballs _____ 5 to 6 servings
Total Cooking Time: 18 to 19 minutes

1 pound lean ground beef
½ cup quick-cooking rice
¼ cup instant minced onion
2 tablespoons minced green pepper
1 egg, slightly beaten
1 teaspoon salt
⅛ teaspoon freshly ground pepper
1 can (10¾ ounces) condensed cream of tomato soup
1 cup water

In small mixing bowl, combine beef, rice, onion, green pepper, egg, salt, and pepper; blend thoroughly. Form into 24 1-inch balls. Arrange in 2-quart microproof casserole. Blend soup and water; pour over meatballs. Cover. Use COOK cycle and cook 18 to 19 minutes, or until beef is no longer red and rice is tender, rearranging meatballs once during cooking time. Let stand 3 minutes. Remove meatballs with slotted spoon. Pour a small amount of sauce over meatballs. Pass remaining sauce, if desired.

Spicy Stuffed Peppers ——————— 5 servings

Total Cooking Time: 30 to 32 minutes

5 green peppers, tops removed and seeded
¾ pound lean ground beef
1 cup quick-cooking rice
¼ cup finely chopped onion
½ teaspoon salt
¼ teaspoon freshly ground pepper
¼ teaspoon garlic powder
1 can (8 ounces) tomato sauce
5 slices sharp Cheddar cheese

Arrange peppers in 8-cup microproof ring mold or 10-inch microproof pie plate. Combine remaining ingredients, except tomato sauce and cheese; blend thoroughly. Divide meat mixture among peppers. Pour tomato sauce over peppers. Cover with plastic wrap. Use COOK cycle and cook 30 to 32 minutes, or until peppers are tender and beef is no longer red. Remove plastic wrap; top each pepper with cheese slice. Return plastic wrap. Let stand 10 minutes before serving.

Salisbury Steak ——————— 4 servings

Total Cooking Time: 20 to 22 minutes

1¼ pounds lean ground beef
1 package (¾ ounce) brown gravy mix
¾ cup water
2 tablespoons catsup
1 teaspoon Worcestershire sauce
1 teaspoon instant minced onion
½ teaspoon salt
⅛ teaspoon freshly ground pepper

Shape ground beef into 4 patties. Place browning dish in oven. Use COOK cycle and cook 10 minutes. Place patties on dish. Use COOK cycle and cook 4 minutes, turning patties after 2 minutes; drain. Combine gravy mix, water, catsup, Worcestershire, and onion. Pour sauce over patties. Cover. Use COOK cycle and cook 6 to 8 minutes, or until patties are desired doneness. Sprinkle with salt and pepper. Serve hot.

Super Meat Loaf Ring ———————— 6 to 8 servings
Total Cooking Time: 22 to 24 minutes

2 pounds lean ground beef
2 eggs, slightly beaten
2 slices fresh white bread, crumbed
1 envelope onion soup mix
2 tablespoons milk
1 teaspoon prepared mustard
1 tablespoon minced fresh parsley
1 can (8 ounces) tomato sauce, divided

Topping

1 tablespoon brown sugar
1 tablespoon vinegar

In large bowl, combine all ingredients, except tomato sauce. Add ¼ cup tomato sauce to meat mixture; mix thoroughly. Spoon into 4- or 5-cup ring mold (check yours to be certain it will fit your oven). Use COOK cycle and cook 20 to 22 minutes, rotating every 10 minutes. Meat loaf ring is done when it pulls away from side of mold. Let stand 5 minutes; drain. Invert onto warmed serving platter.

To prepare Topping, mix sugar, remaining tomato sauce, and vinegar in 2-cup glass measure. Use COOK cycle and cook 2 minutes. Stir. Pour half of sauce over meat loaf ring. Serve remaining sauce as gravy.

As a serving suggestion, fill meatloaf ring with hot vegetables such as Brussels sprouts, chopped broccoli, carrots, peas, etc.

If you prefer, brush ring with soy sauce before and after cooking. Omit Topping.

Super Meatloaf Ring (variation), String Beans (Guide, page 64)→

Pot Roast and Vegetables ———— 4 to 6 servings
Total Cooking Time: 70 to 75 minutes

3 tablespoons all-purpose flour
½ teaspoon salt
½ teaspoon dry mustard
½ teaspoon garlic powder
¼ teaspoon freshly ground pepper
½ cup catsup
½ cup water
1 tablespoon Worcestershire sauce
1 boneless chuck roast (3 to 4 pounds), fat trimmed
3 medium potatoes, peeled and halved
2 medium carrots, cut into 2-inch pieces
3 small onions, cut in half

Cut 1-inch strip from open end of 14×20-inch cooking bag; reserve strip and set aside. In small bowl, combine flour, salt, mustard, garlic powder, and pepper. Stir in catsup, water and Worcestershire.

Place roast in bag. Spoon seasoning mixture evenly over roast. Add potatoes, carrots, and onions. Turn bag to distribute liquid. Secure end of bag with reserved strip. Place bag in appropriate size microproof baking dish. Use COOK cycle and cook 30 minutes. Turn bag over. Use COOK cycle and cook 20 minutes. If mixture becomes too dry, add small amount of water. Use DEFROST cycle and cook 20 to 25 minutes, or until meat reaches desired doneness and vegetables are tender. Let stand in bag 10 minutes before serving.

Louisiana Pepper Steak ———— 4 servings
Total Cooking Time: 30 minutes

1 pound round steak, cut in ¼×1-inch strips
1 can (10¾ ounces) beef broth
2 medium green peppers, seeded and cut in strips
¼ cup water
3 tablespoons cornstarch
1 tablespoon steak sauce
1 medium tomato, cut in wedges

In 8-inch round microproof casserole, combine steak and broth. Use COOK cycle and cook 20 minutes, or until steak is tender. Add green pepper. Cover with plastic wrap. Use COOK cycle and cook 7 minutes. Combine water, cornstarch, and steak sauce; stir to dissolve cornstarch. Add to steak and peppers. Arrange tomato wedges on top. Use COOK cycle and cook 3 minutes. Serve over hot cooked rice, if desired.

Simmered Corned Beef ——————— 8 to 10 servings
Total Cooking Time: 80 to 90 minutes

1 corned beef brisket (3 to 3½ pounds)
1½ cups water
2 cloves garlic, halved
2 bay leaves
4 peppercorns
1 large onion, sliced

In 3-quart microproof casserole, combine brisket, water, garlic, bay leaves, and peppercorns. Arrange sliced onion over brisket. Cover. Use COOK cycle and cook 30 minutes; turn brisket. Cover. Use DEFROST cycle and cook 50 to 60 minutes, or until brisket is tender, turning after 25 minutes. Add more water, if necessary. Let stand in liquid 15 minutes. Cut in thin slices across the grain.

Leftover Meat Stew ——————— 5 to 6 servings
Total Cooking Time: 42 to 45 minutes

2 to 3 cups cubed beef, pork, or lamb
4 medium carrots, peeled and sliced
3 medium potatoes, peeled and cubed
1 medium onion, quartered
1 cup water
1 package (¾ ounce) mushroom gravy mix
1 teaspoon Worcestershire sauce
1 teaspoon salt
⅛ teaspoon freshly ground pepper
1 cup fresh or frozen peas
Minced fresh parsley

Combine all ingredients, except peas and parsley, in 3-quart microproof casserole. Cover. Use COOK cycle and cook 37 to 40 minutes, or until vegetables are tender, stirring every 10 minutes. Stir in peas. Cover. Use DEFROST cycle and cook 5 minutes. Sprinkle with parsley. Let stand 5 minutes before serving.

The following mixtures can be substituted for the mushroom gravy mix: 1½ cups leftover gravy mixed with ¼ cup water, or 1 can (10¾ ounces) condensed cream of celery soup mixed with ¾ cup water.

Polynesian Pork Kabobs ——————— 4 servings
Total Cooking Time: 9 minutes

½ cup bottled teriyaki
   marinade
2 tablespoons honey
1 teaspoon vinegar
½ pound pork tenderloin,
   cut into 16 1-inch cubes
1 small green pepper,
   seeded and cut in
   squares
1 can (8 ounces) pineapple
   chunks, drained,
   syrup reserved
8 large mushrooms, stems
   removed
8 cherry tomatoes

In 1-quart glass measure, mix marinade, honey, and vinegar. Add pork cubes; stir to coat. Cover with waxed paper. Use COOK cycle and cook 6 minutes, stirring halfway through cooking time. Set aside to cool. Thread pork, green pepper squares, mushrooms, pineapple chunks, and cherry tomatoes on wooden or bamboo skewers, repeating until full. Arrange on 10- or 11-inch microproof plate in spoke fashion with tomatoes in center. Brush with marinade.
   Use COOK cycle and cook 3 minutes, or until vegetables are crisp-tender, turning skewers once during cooking time. Cover and let stand 2 minutes. Serve with hot cooked rice seasoned with curry, if desired.

Spareribs in
Barbecue Sauce ————————————— 4 servings
Total Cooking Time: 40 to 42 minutes

2 pounds lean spareribs,
   cut in serving pieces
1 can (8 ounces) tomato
   sauce
¼ cup firmly packed brown
   sugar
¼ cup cider vinegar
2 tablespoons instant
   minced onion
1 tablespoon horseradish
1 tablespoon Worcestershire
   sauce
1 clove garlic, minced
½ teaspoon salt
½ teaspoon dry mustard
⅛ teaspoon turmeric

Arrange ribs in 2-quart microproof casserole. In small bowl, combine remaining ingredients; blend well. Pour sauce over ribs. Cover. Use COOK cycle and cook 15 minutes; turn ribs. Cover. Use COOK cycle and cook 15 minutes; rearrange ribs. Cover. Use DEFROST cycle and cook 10 to 12 minutes, or until ribs are tender. Let stand 3 minutes before serving.

Polynesian Pork Kabobs→

Sauced Pork Chops ———————— 4 servings
Total Cooking Time: 28 to 31 minutes

4 center loin pork chops
  (about ¾ inch thick)
¼ teaspoon salt
¼ teaspoon freshly ground
  pepper
1 can (11 ounces) mandarin
  oranges, drained,
  liquid reserved
½ cup chopped chutney
2 tablespoons lemon juice
1 tablespoon sugar
1 tablespoon cornstarch

Arrange pork chops in 8-inch round microproof baking dish placing thickest portions toward outside of dish. Sprinkle with salt and pepper. Cover with waxed paper. Use COOK cycle and cook 15 minutes; drain; turn chops over. Mix ⅓ cup reserved orange liquid with chutney, sugar, and lemon juice. Arrange orange sections over pork chops. Top with chutney mixture. Cover. Use COOK cycle and cook 10 to 12 minutes, or until thoroughly done. Remove chops to warmed serving platter. Cover to keep warm.

Mix cornstarch and 2 tablespoons orange liquid. Stir into juices in dish. Use COOK cycle and cook 3 to 4 minutes, or until thickened and smooth, stirring twice during cooking. Spoon over chops.

Sliced Ham with Cherries ———— 6 to 8 servings
Total Cooking Time: 20½ minutes

¼ cup Burgundy
¼ cup firmly packed brown
  sugar
2 tablespoons butter or
  margarine
¼ teaspoon ginger
¼ teaspoon cloves
1 slice (1½ pounds)
  cooked ham
1 cup cherry pie filling

In 11 × 8 × 2-inch oval glass baking dish, mix wine, sugar, butter, ginger and cloves. Use COOK cycle and cook 1½ minutes, or until butter is melted and sugar dissolved. Stir. Add ham; turn to coat. Cover with waxed paper. Use COOK cycle and cook 15 minutes, or until heated through. Remove ham to serving platter. Add cherry pie filling to sauce; stir. Cover. Use COOK cycle and cook 4 minutes, or until thick and heated through. Pour sauce over ham and serve.

If using fresh ham, use COOK cycle and cook 30 minutes.

Party Ham Loaf _____ 4 to 6 servings
Total Cooking Time: 15 minutes

2 cups coarsely ground
   cooked ham
1 cup finely crushed
   cracker crumbs
1 can (20 ounces) crushed
   pineapple, drained,
   syrup reserved
1 egg
1 teaspoon onion flakes
½ teaspoon dry mustard

In mixing bowl, combine ham, crumbs, ½ cup reserved syrup, egg, onion, and mustard. Line 4-cup microproof ring mold with pineapple. Spoon ham mixture evenly over pineapple, pressing lightly into mold. Use COOK cycle and cook 15 minutes. Invert onto serving platter. Center of mold can be filled with cooked green vegetables before serving.

Tavern Franks _____ 8 servings
Total Cooking Time: 10 to 12 minutes

1 pound (8 to 10)
   frankfurters
1 small onion, thinly sliced
1½ cups beer (12 ounces)

Place frankfurters in 2-quart microproof casserole. Separate onion into rings; spread over frankfurters. Pour beer over all. Cover. Use COOK cycle and cook 10 to 12 minutes, or until heated through. After 5 minutes, rearrange frankfurters to bring those on the bottom to the top. Serve with or without buns.

For fuller flavor, marinate uncooked frankfurters overnight in beer before cooking.

Lamb Stew with Beans ———————— 4 servings

Total Cooking Time: 30 to 32 minutes

1 pound lamb steak, cut
   in cubes
2 cups water, divided
2 tablespoons cornstarch
½ teaspocn salt
¼ teaspoon freshly ground
   pepper
¼ teaspoon Worcestershire
   sauce
1 medium potato, peeled
   and cubed
2 medium carrots, thinly
   sliced
1 stalk celery, thinly
   sliced
1 small onion, diced
½ cup fresh lima beans
¼ cup white wine (optional)
1 teaspoon parsley flakes
¼ teaspoon thyme

Combine lamb, cornstarch, 1 cup of the water, salt, pepper, and Worcestershire in 2-quart microproof bowl. Use COOK cycle and cook 10 minutes. Stir in remaining 1 cup water. Add remaining ingredients. Cover with plastic wrap. Use COOK cycle and cook 20 to 22 minutes, or until vegetables are tender. Let stand 5 minutes before serving.

POULTRY PLATTERS

Plain, crumb-coated, soy brushed, barbecue-sauced, and honey-glazed chicken breasts (right). Microwave thermometers take the guessing out of cooking whole poultry (above).

Still about our most economical food, chicken is more juicy, flavorful, and tender than ever when cooked in the microwave oven. It is a special favorite of microwave cooks because it requires less attention than most main dish meat. Duck and Cornish hen are great, too, as is turkey, though you'll need to select a small turkey that fits in your oven or prepare turkey parts.

Poultry turns out golden brown, though not dark brown or crisp. If you are a crisp-skin lover, the microwave oven is still for you. Simply crisp the skin in a conventional oven at 450°F for 5 or 10 minutes, after the microwave cooking time. And how about this time-saving twist for charcoal grilling: you can avoid the long time delays by partially cooking poultry in the microwave oven, then finishing it on the grill! Full charcoal-grilled flavor is retained. Try our recipes, then adapt your own favorites.

← *Arrange chicken pieces with thickest portions along edge of dish.*

Converting Your Recipes

Conventional one-dish poultry recipes that call for cut-up pieces are easy to adapt for the microwave oven. You are sure to find a similar recipe in this chapter to use as a guide. Here, too, are some tips to follow:

☐ Use care in selecting whole poultry. Chances are your oven will not be able to manage a whole turkey. (Even the largest microwave ovens cannot accommodate a turkey larger than 12 to 14 pounds.)
☐ Conventional pop-up indicators for doneness do not work correctly in the microwave oven.
☐ When using a microwave meat thermometer, insert it in the fleshy part of the inside thigh muscle, without touching the bone.
☐ Standing time is essential to complete cooking. Allow up to 15 minutes standing time for whole poultry depending upon size. The internal temperature will rise approximately 15°F during 15 minutes standing time. Chicken pieces and casseroles need only 5 minutes standing time.

The Defrosting Guide

1. Poultry can begin defrosting within the original paper or plastic wrapping. However, it will defrost more evenly if removed from wrappings as soon as possible. Remove all metal rings, wire twist ties, and any aluminum foil. The metal leg clamps need not be removed until after defrosting. Be careful, of course, that the metal is at least 1 inch from the oven walls.

2. Place poultry in microproof dish while defrosting.

3. Defrost only as long as necessary. Poultry should be cool in the center when removed from the oven.

4. To speed defrosting during standing time, poultry may be placed in cold water.

5. Separate chicken pieces as soon as partially thawed.

6. Wing and leg tips and area near breastbone may begin cooking before center is thoroughly defrosted. When these areas appear thawed, cover them with small strips of aluminum foil; this foil should be at least 1 inch from oven walls.

DEFROSTING GUIDE — POULTRY

Food	Amount	Minutes (per pound)	Control	Standing Time (minutes)	Special Notes
Capon	6 - 8 lbs.	2½	COOK	60	Turn over once. Immerse in cold water for standing time.
Chicken, cut up	2 - 3 lbs.	5 - 6	DEFROST	10 - 15	Turn every 5 minutes. Separate pieces when partially thawed.
Chicken, whole	2 - 3 lbs.	6 - 8	DEFROST	25 - 30	Turn over once. Immerse in cold water for standing time.
Cornish hens	1, 1 - 1½ lbs. 2, 1 - 1½ lbs. ea.	12 - 13 20 - 21	DEFROST DEFROST	20 20	Turn over once.
Duckling	4 - 5 lbs.	5	COOK	30 - 40	Turn over once. Immerse in cold water for standing time.
Turkey	Under 8 lbs. Over 8 lbs.	3 - 5 3 - 5	DEFROST COOK	60 60	Turn over once. Immerse in cold water for standing time.
Turkey breast	Under 4 lbs. Over 4 lbs.	3 - 5 3½	DEFROST COOK	20 20	Turn over once.
Turkey drumsticks	1 - 1½ lbs.	5 - 6	DEFROST	15 - 20	Turn every 5 minutes. Separate pieces when partially thawed.
Turkey roast, boneless	2 - 4 lbs.	3 - 4	DEFROST	10	Remove from foil pan. Cover with waxed paper.

Using the Cooking Guide

1. Defrost frozen poultry completely before cooking.
2. Remove giblets and rinse poultry in cool water, then pat dry.
3. When cooking whole birds, place on a microproof roasting rack or an inverted microproof saucer in a glass baking dish large enough to catch drippings.
4. Turn over, as directed in Guide, halfway through cooking time.
5. Cook whole poultry covered loosely with a waxed paper tent to prevent splattering. Toward end of cooking time, small pieces of aluminum foil may be used to cover legs, wing tips, or breastbone area to prevent overcooking. Foil should be at least 1 inch from oven walls.
6. Cover poultry pieces with glass lid or plastic wrap during cooking.
7. Standing time completes the cooking of poultry. Cooked whole birds may be covered with aluminum foil during standing time.

COOKING GUIDE — POULTRY
Use COOK cycle.

Food	First Cook Time (minutes)	Second Cook Time (minutes)	Standing Time (minutes)	Special Notes
Chicken, whole, 2 - 3 pounds	4 - 5 per pound	Turn over. 5 - 6 per pound	5 (covered with foil)	Shallow baking dish, roasting rack, breast up.
3 - 5 pounds	5 per pound	Turn over. 5 - 6 per pound	5	6 × 9-inch baking dish, roasting rack, breast up.
Chicken, cut up 2½ - 3½ pounds	5 per pound	Turn over. 5 per pound	5	6 × 9-inch baking dish. Cover.
Chicken, quartered	4 - 5 per pound	Turn over. 4 - 5 per pound	5	Shallow baking dish, skin side down.
Cornish hens 1 - 1½ pounds	5 per pound	Turn over. 4 per pound	5	Shallow baking dish, breast down. Cover.
Duckling 4 - 5 pounds	4½ per pound	Turn over. Drain excess fat. 4 - 5 per pound	8 - 10	Shallow baking dish, roasting rack. Cover.
Turkey, whole, 8 - 14 pounds	6½ - 7 per pound	Turn over. 4½ - 5 per pound	10 - 15 (covered with foil)	Shallow baking dish, 6 × 9-inch, roasting rack, breast up.
Turkey breast, 3 - 4 pounds	9 - 9½ per pound	Turn over. 5½ - 6 per pound		Shallow baking dish, roasting rack.
Turkey roast, boneless 2 - 4 pounds	11 per pound	Turn over. 10 per pound	10 - 15	Loaf pan. Cover with plastic wrap.
Turkey parts, 2 - 3 pounds	8 - 9 per pound	Turn over. 8 - 9 per pound	5	Shallow baking dish with roasting rack.

West Indian Chicken _____ 6 to 8 servings

Total Cooking Time: 42 to 44 minutes

1 tablespoon butter or margarine
6 to 8 chicken thighs, skinned
1 cup minced onion
2 tablespoons lemon juice
1 tablespoon brown sugar
½ teaspoon salt
1 cup chopped tomato
2 tablespoons raisins
1 teaspoon oregano
½ teaspoon thyme
1 teaspoon Worcestershire sauce
2 tablespoons sweet vermouth
2 cups hot cooked rice

Place browning dish in oven. Use COOK cycle and heat 10 minutes. Add butter. When butter is melted, quickly add chicken thighs to brown. Use COOK cycle and cook 4 minutes. Turn chicken. Add onion and lemon juice; sprinkle sugar and salt over chicken. Cover. Use COOK cycle and cook 8 to 10 minutes, or until onion is tender. Add tomato, raisins, oregano, thyme, Worcestershire, and vermouth. Cover. Use DEFROST cycle and cook 20 minutes, or until chicken is tender and all ingredients are blended. Serve with rice.

COOKING GUIDE — CONVENIENCE POULTRY

Food	Amount	Control	Time (minutes)	Special Notes
Precooked breaded chicken, frozen	1 piece 2 pieces 4 pieces 2 - 3 lbs.	COOK	1½ - 2 2½ - 3 3 - 3½ 12 - 14	Remove wrapping and place in microproof baking dish.
Chicken Kiev, frozen	1 piece 2 pieces	DEFROST COOK DEFROST COOK	4 - 5 3 - 4 6 - 7 5½ - 6½	Remove plastic wrap, place on microproof plate. First, thaw on DEFROST and then, cook on COOK.
Chicken à la King, frozen	5 oz.	COOK	4 - 5	Place on microproof plate. Stir before serving.
Creamed Chicken, Chicken and Dumplings, canned	7½ - 10½ oz.	COOK	2½ - 5	Stir once.
Escalloped chicken, chow mein, canned	14 - 24 oz.	COOK	5 - 6½	Stir halfway through cooking time.
Turkey tetrazzini, frozen	12 oz.	COOK	3½ - 5	Place on microproof plate. Stir before serving.
Turkey, sliced in gravy, frozen	5 oz.	COOK	3½ - 6½	Place in microproof dish. Make slit in pouch before heating.

Oven Baked Chicken ———————— 4 to 6 servings
Total Cooking Time: 37 to 40 minutes

2½ to 3-pound frying
    chicken, cut up
⅓ cup sherry
1 envelope (2⅜ ounces)
    seasoned coating mix
    for chicken

Wash chicken and pat dry with paper towels. Dip in sherry. Place seasoned coating mix in plastic bag. Shake a few pieces of chicken at a time until coated. Arrange in 10-inch round microproof dish, skin-side up, with thickest portions toward outside of dish. Cover with paper towels. Use COOK cycle and cook 37 to 40 minutes, or until chicken is tender. Let stand 5 minutes before serving.

For crisper and browner chicken, do not cover. If splattering occurs, cover lightly with paper towels.

To reduce calories, substitute chicken bouillon for sherry.

Chicken Tetrazzini _____ 4 to 6 servings
Total Cooking Time: 17 to 22 minutes

2 ounces uncooked spaghetti, broken into 2-inch pieces
1 tablespoon butter or margarine
⅓ cup minced onion
¼ pound mushrooms, sliced
1½ tablespoons all-purpose flour
1 cup chicken broth
¼ cup light cream or half-and-half
⅛ cup dry vermouth
½ cup grated Parmesan cheese, divided
¼ teaspoon salt
Dash white pepper
1 cup diced cooked chicken
1 tablespoon minced fresh parsley

Cook spaghetti according to package directions. Drain immediately; rinse in cold water to stop cooking; set aside.

In 1½-quart microproof casserole, place butter, onion, and mushrooms. Cover. Use COOK cycle and cook 3 to 4 minutes, or until onion is transparent. Stir in flour to make a paste.

In 4-cup glass measure, combine broth, cream, and vermouth. Use COOK cycle and cook 3 minutes; slowly stir into flour mixture; blend thoroughly. Stir in ¼ cup cheese, salt, and pepper; blend well. Use COOK cycle and cook 8 to 12 minutes, or until mixture comes to a boil and thickens, stirring once during cooking time.

Carefully stir in cooked spaghetti, chicken, and remaining cheese. Cover. Use COOK cycle and cook 3 minutes. Let stand, covered, 5 minutes before serving. Sprinkle with parsley.

Turkey can be substituted for chicken. This recipe can be easily doubled.

Onion-Glazed Chicken _____ 6 servings
Total Cooking Time: 30 to 32 minutes

1 bottle (8 ounces) Russian salad dressing
1 can (11 ounces) mandarin orange segments, drained
1 envelope onion soup mix
1 2 to 2½-pound frying chicken, cut into serving pieces

In small bowl, mix dressing, orange segments, and soup mix. Arrange chicken in 1½-quart microproof casserole. Pour sauce over chicken. Cover with waxed paper. Use COOK cycle and cook 30 to 32 minutes, or until chicken is tender, rotating dish once during cooking time.

Halved Cornish Hens ——————— 4 servings

Total Cooking Time: 23 to 24 minutes

2 Cornish hens (1 pound,
6 ounces each), halved
lengthwise
5 tablespoons dry vermouth,
divided
1 envelope seasoned
coating mix for
chicken
1 teaspoon thyme
4 canned peach halves,
drained

Rinse Cornish hen halves; pat dry with paper towels. Brush on all sides with 1/4 cup of the vermouth. Blend coating mix with thyme in a plastic bag. Shake 1 hen half at a time in plastic bag until thoroughly coated.

Arrange halves, skin side up, with thickest portion toward outside of a 10-inch microproof pie plate. Cover with waxed paper. Use COOK cycle and cook 20 to 21 minutes, or until tender.

Place peach halves, cut side up, in center of pie plate. Divide remaining vermouth among centers of peaches. Cover with waxed paper. Use COOK cycle and cook 3 minutes, or until peaches are warm.

Cracker or cornflake crumbs can be used in place of seasoned coating mix.

Swiss Chicken and Ham Roll-Ups ——————————— 6 servings

Total Cooking Time: 12 to 14 minutes

1½ cups coarsely ground
   cooked chicken
1 can (10¾ ounces)
   condensed cream of
   chicken soup, divided
1 green onion, thinly
   sliced
6 slices boiled ham
2 cups cooked rice
¼ cup dairy sour cream or
   yogurt
¼ cup milk
½ cup shredded Swiss cheese
   Paprika

In mixing bowl, combine chicken, ⅓ cup soup, and onion. Spoon ¼ cup chicken mixture on each ham slice and roll up. Secure with wooden toothpick, if necessary. Spread rice in shallow 1½-quart microproof dish. Place roll-ups on top of rice. Mix remaining soup with sour cream and milk. Pour over ham rolls. Use COOK cycle and cook 12 to 14 minutes. Sprinkle with cheese and paprika. Cover and let stand 5 minutes before serving.

Mandarin Chicken and Rice ———— 4 servings

Total Cooking Time: 27 minutes

1 can (16 ounces) chop suey
   vegetables, drained
1 can (10¾ ounces)
   condensed cream of
   mushroom soup
¾ cup quick-cooking rice
1 can (5.3 ounces)
   evaporated milk
1 can (4 ounces) mushroom
   pieces, undrained
¼ cup minced onion
2 whole chicken breasts,
   boned and halved
   Paprika

In 3-quart microproof casserole, blend vegetables, soup, rice, milk, mushrooms with liquid, and onion. Cover. Use COOK cycle and cook 7 minutes, stirring halfway through cooking time. Arrange chicken breasts on top of casserole, placing thickest parts toward outside of casserole. Cover. Use COOK cycle and cook 20 minutes, or until tender. Sprinkle with paprika. Let stand, covered, 5 minutes before serving.

Micro-Fried Chicken Steaks ——————— 4 patties
Total Cooking Time: 15½ to 17 minutes

1½ cups fresh bread crumbs
1 cup cooked chicken meat, chopped
⅓ cup milk
2 tablespoons chopped onion
1 tablespoon minced fresh parsley
¼ teaspoon salt
⅛ teaspoon pepper
½ teaspoon paprika
White Sauce (page 73)

In a 1½ quart bowl, combine 1 cup bread crumbs, chicken, milk, onion, parsley, salt, and pepper. Form into 4 patties. Mix paprika with remaining bread crumbs. Coat patties with crumb mixture. Place in 9-inch or 10-inch round microproof plate. Use COOK cycle and cook 4 minutes; turn patties over and continue to cook 3 to 4 minutes. Top with White Sauce. Sprinkle with remaining bread crumbs.

Chicken Breasts with Cashews ——— 4 servings
Total Cooking Time: 25 to 28 minutes

1 package (6 ounces) frozen pea pods
2 tablespoons dry white wine or water
1 tablespoon soy sauce
1 tablespoon oil
1 tablespoon cornstarch
⅛ teaspoon pepper
⅛ teaspoon hot sauce
2 whole boneless chicken breasts, skinned and flattened to ¼ inch thickness
1 medium onion, sliced into rings
1 red or green pepper, sliced into strips
2 tablespoons oil
1 cup whole cashews, unsalted
½ cup chicken stock or bouillon

Use DEFROST cycle and defrost pea pods for 5 minutes. Set aside. In a small bowl, combine wine, soy sauce, oil, cornstarch, pepper and hot sauce. Cut each whole chicken breast into 4 to 6 pieces. Add each piece to wine marinade, then place chicken in a 9 or 10 inch microproof pie plate. Pour remaining marinade over pieces, allow to marinate 15 to 20 minutes. In a 2 quart microproof bowl, combine onion, pepper slices, and oil. Use COOK cycle and cook 6 minutes, stirring once. Add cashews and chicken stock. Pour marinade into onion-oil mixture. Stir to blend well. Use COOK cycle and cook chicken pieces for 4 minutes. Turn pieces over and rearrange. Use COOK cycle and cook 2 to 3 minutes, or until chicken loses its pink color. Cover and set aside. Use COOK cycle and cook sauce mixture, covered, 6 to 7 minutes, or until thickened. Stir in pea pods. Spoon sauce over chicken. Use COOK cycle and cook 2 to 3 minutes, or until heated through. Serve over hot cooked rice.

Wagonwheel Drumsticks Dinner ____ 2 servings

Total Cooking Time: 28 to 30 minutes

4 chicken legs (about
  1 pound)
2 tablespoons Italian salad
  dressing
¼ cup Italian seasoned
  bread crumbs
2 8-ounce potatoes, cut in
  half lengthwise
2 tablespoons butter, melted
¼ cup Parmesan cheese
  Paprika

Coat chicken legs with Italian dressing and bread crumbs. Place in a 10-inch round microproof plate in spoke fashion, with meaty portion of leg on the outer edges. Place a potato half between each leg, skin side down. Brush with butter and Parmesan cheese. Sprinkle with paprika. Cover with paper towel. Use COOK cycle and cook 15 minutes, rotating dish once. Turn legs over and turn potatoes around. Use COOK cycle and cook 13 to 15 minutes, or until legs are done, turning dish once.

Turkey Breast with Wild Rice Stuffing _____ 4 to 6 servings

Total Cooking Time: 59 to 64 minutes

1 medium onion, sliced
¾ cup celery, sliced
2 tablespoons butter or
  margarine
1 cup mushrooms, sliced
2½ cups wild rice, cooked
  (Guide, page 63)
½ cup almonds
¼ cup chopped fresh
  parsley
1 teaspoon poultry seasoning
2 slices bread ends
3 to 4 pound whole turkey
  breast (cleaned, rinsed
  and patted dry)
  Vegetable oil
  Paprika

In 2-quart glass measure, combine onion, celery, and butter. Use COOK cycle and cook 6 minutes. Stir in mushrooms. Use COOK cycle and cook 3 minutes. Stir in rice, almonds, parsley, and poultry seasoning. Stuff neck cavity and fold over skin. Secure with wooden skewer or toothpicks. Fill large cavity with remaining stuffing. Cover stuffing with bread ends and tie breast with string to hold bread in place over stuffing. Rub skin with oil and sprinkle with paprika. Set trivet or small microproof rack into glass or ceramic baking dish. Place breast, skin side down, on trivet. Use COOK cycle and cook 30 minutes, turning dish once. Turn breast over. Use COOK cycle and cook 20 to 25 minutes, or until done (170°F on a microproof food thermometer). Let stand 10 minutes before serving.

Bread Stuffing (below) may be substituted for Wild Rice Stuffing. Cooking time remains the same.

Bread Stuffing _____ 6 servings

Total Cooking Time: 10 minutes

¼ cup butter or margarine
⅓ cup chopped onion
¼ cup chopped celery
3 cups dry bread cubes
1 cup chicken broth or
  water
2 teaspoons parsley flakes
½ teaspoon salt
⅛ teaspoon freshly ground
  pepper

Combine butter, onion, and celery in 4-cup glass measure. Use COOK cycle and cook 10 minutes, or until onion is transparent. Stir in remaining ingredients. Makes enough stuffing for 5- to 6-pound roasting chicken.

←*Turkey Breast with Wild Rice Stuffing*

Brunswick Stew ———————— 4 to 6 servings
Total Cooking Time: 30 minutes

2¼ cups water, divided
2 cups cubed uncooked
  chicken
2 chicken bouillon cubes
1 teaspoon parsley flakes
4 peppercorns
1 cup thinly sliced carrots
¼ cup sliced celery
1 medium onion, diced
5 medium mushrooms, sliced
  (about ½ cup)
3 tablespoons cornstarch

In 2-quart microproof bowl, combine 2 cups water, chicken, boullion, parsley, and peppercorns. Use COOK cycle and cook 15 minutes. Add carrots, celery, onion, and mushrooms; mix lightly. Combine ¼ cup water and cornstarch; stir to dissolve cornstarch. Add to chicken and vegetables. Cover with plastic wrap. Use COOK cycle and cook 15 minutes, or until vegetables are tender. Let stand, covered, 10 minutes before serving.

Chicken Liver Chow Mein ———— 4 to 6 servings
Total Cooking Time: 24 to 26 minutes

½ pound chicken livers,
  rinsed and drained
3 tablespoons butter or
  margarine, divided
½ cup sliced celery
¼ cup chopped onion
1 envelope (1¾ ounces)
  mushroom gravy mix
1 can (16 ounces) Chinese
  vegetables
1 can (8 ounces) sliced
  water chestnuts,
  drained
1 tablespoon soy sauce
2 cups cooked rice
  Chow mein noodles

Pierce chicken livers in several places with a toothpick. Combine livers with 2 tablespoons of the butter in 4-cup glass measure. Cover. Use COOK cycle and cook 6 to 8 minutes, or until livers are no longer pink, stirring once during cooking time. Drain and set aside.

In 3-quart microproof casserole, mix remaining 1 tablespoon butter with celery and onion. Cover. Use COOK cycle and cook 5 minutes, or until onion is transparent. Stir in gravy mix. Add Chinese vegetables, water chestnuts, and soy sauce; stir lightly. Cover. Use COOK cycle and cook 10 minutes, or until heated through. Cut livers into bite-size pieces. Add to vegetables, stirring carefully. Use COOK cycle and cook 3 minutes. Let stand covered 5 minutes. Serve over rice. Sprinkle with chow mein noodles.

Turkey Crunch ——————————— 6 servings
Total Cooking Time: 20 minutes

1 tablespoon butter or margarine
1/4 cup sliced celery
1/4 cup chopped onion
1/4 cup chopped green pepper
1 can (10¾ ounces) condensed cream of mushroom soup
1/4 cup milk
1 can (5 ounces) chow mein noodles
1½ cups diced cooked turkey or chicken
1 can (4 ounces) mushroom pieces, drained
2 tablespoons sliced pimiento
1/4 teaspoon poultry seasoning
1/4 teaspoon salt

Combine butter, celery, onion, and green pepper in 2-quart microproof casserole. Use COOK cycle and cook 7 minutes, or until vegetables are tender, stirring once during cooking time. In small bowl, combine soup and milk; stir into onion mixture. Stir in 2 cups chow mein noodles, turkey, mushrooms, pimiento, poultry seasoning, and salt. Use COOK cycle and cook 12 minutes. Stir. Sprinkle remaining noodles around edges of casserole. Use COOK cycle and cook 1 minute. Let stand 2 minutes before serving.

Glazed Turkey Legs ——————— 2 to 4 servings
Total Cooking Time: 36½ to 37 minutes

2 turkey legs (2½ to 3 pounds)
1/3 cup honey
1 teaspoon grated lemon peel
1 teaspoon lemon juice
1 teaspoon cornstarch
1/4 teaspoon bottled brown sauce

Place turkey legs in 10-inch round microproof dish; cover with paper towel. Use COOK cycle and cook 15 minutes, turning once. Turn legs over. Use COOK cycle and cook 15 minutes. In a small bowl, combine honey, lemon peel, lemon juice, cornstarch, and brown sauce. Use COOK cycle and cook 1½ to 2 minutes, or until thick. Brush turkey legs with half of the glaze. Use COOK cycle and cook 2½ minutes. Turn legs over; brush with remaining glaze. Use COOK cycle and cook 2½ minutes.

Orange-Glazed Duckling ——————— 4 servings

Total Cooking Time: 54 to 54½ minutes

1 duckling (3 to 4 pounds),
  quartered
Salt
Freshly ground pepper
¾ cup fresh orange juice
2 tablespoons sugar
2 teaspoons cornstarch
1 tablespoon grated fresh
  orange peel
½ teaspoon garlic powder
1 small orange, sectioned
  and each section
  quartered
2 tablespoons dry sherry

Sprinkle both sides of duckling with salt and pepper. Pierce skin in several places with fork. Place, skin side up, in shallow oval 10×7×2-inch microproof baking dish with thickest portions toward outside of dish. Cover with waxed paper. Use COOK cycle and cook 30 minutes, covering wings with 1-inch strip of aluminum foil halfway through cooking time. Drain; rearrange pieces, skin side down. Cover. Use COOK cycle and cook 10 minutes. Turn pieces skin side up. Cover. Use DEFROST cycle and cook 10 minutes, or until tender.

Combine juice, sugar, cornstarch, orange peel, and garlic powder in 2-cup glass measure. Use COOK cycle and cook 4 to 4½ minutes, or until thickened, stirring every minute. Stir in orange sections and sherry. Arrange duck on serving platter. Pour half of sauce over duck. Pass remaining sauce.

SEAFOOD SAMPLER

Fish fillets cook best when rolled and arranged around the outside of the dish (left). Fish steaks are arranged as close to a round pattern as possible (above).

In microwave cooking, there's fast and then there's *fast* — seafood cooking. If you have been impressed with the cooking speed of your oven for chicken and other food, you'll be amazed at its performance with fish. For best results, have everything ready and then cook your fish last. Even standing time is short.

Seafood from the microwave oven is a quality success, too. It is so moist, tender, and delicious that you'll never want to cook it any other way. The results are truly as good as if the most accomplished French chef had paid a visit to your kitchen!

Keep in mind that fish is versatile. Most recipes that specify a particular variety will work with many substitutes. When a recipe calls for fish fillets, you can use sole, flounder, bluefish, cod, scrod, perch, or any similar fish. The number one rule in cooking fish: it's done when opaque and barely able to flake.

Converting Your Recipes

As in conventional cooking, the secret to seafood in the microwave oven is to watch it carefully, since fish can overcook in seconds. Other than that, all you need is to refer to a recipe here similar to yours, or find clues in the Guides and these tips:

- ☐ Cook fish covered unless it is coated with crumbs, which seal in the juices.
- ☐ When cooking whole fish, the dish should be rotated one-quarter turn twice during the cooking process to help provide even cooking. The odd shape of the fish requires this procedure.
- ☐ Shellfish is done when flesh is opaque and just firm.
- ☐ Shellfish come in their own cooking containers which respond well to microwave cooking. Clam and mussel shells open before your eyes. Shrimp, crab, and lobster shells turn pink.
- ☐ You can use the browning dish for fillets or fish patties. Preheat, add butter or oil and brown on one side for best results.
- ☐ To remove seafood odors from the oven, combine 1 cup water with lemon juice and cloves in a small microproof bowl. Use COOK cycle and cook 6 to 8 minutes.

Using the Defrosting Guide

1. While frozen fish may be thawed in its original wrapper, it is best to remove wrappings first. Discard any aluminum foil, metal rings, or wire twist ties before defrosting.

2. Place fish on microproof dish. A rack may be used.

3. To prevent the outer edges from drying out or beginning to cook, it is best to remove fish from oven before it has completely thawed.

4. Finish defrosting under cold running water, separating fillets.

DEFROSTING GUIDE — SEAFOOD

Food	Amount	Control	Time (minutes)	Standing Time (minutes)	Special Notes
Fish Fillets	1 lb.	DEFROST	4 - 6	5	Defrost in package on dish.
	2 lbs.	DEFROST	5 - 7	5	Carefully separate fillets under cold water. Turn once.
Fish steaks	1 lb.	DEFROST	4 - 6	5	Defrost in package on dish. Carefully separate steaks under cold running water.
Whole fish	8 - 10 oz.	DEFROST	4 - 6	5	Shallow dish; shape of fish
	1½ - 2 lbs.	DEFROST	5 - 7	5	determines size. Should be icy when removed. Finish at room temperature. Cover head with aluminum foil. Turn once.
Lobster tails	8 oz. package	DEFROST	5 - 7	5	Remove from package to baking dish.
Crab legs	8 - 10 oz.	DEFROST	5 - 7	5	Glass baking dish. Break apart and turn once.
Crabmeat	6 oz.	DEFROST	4 - 5	5	Defrost in package on dish. Break apart. Turn once.
Shrimp	1 lb.	DEFROST	3 - 4	5	Remove from package to dish. Spread loosely in baking dish and rearrange during thawing as necessary.
Scallops	1 lb.	DEFROST	8 - 10	5	Defrost in package if in block; spread out on baking dish if in pieces. Turn over and rearrange during thawing as necessary.
Oysters	12 oz.	DEFROST	3 - 4	5	Remove from package to dish. Turn over and rearrange during thawing as necessary.

Using the Cooking Guide

1. Defrost seafood fully; then cook.
2. Remove original wrapping. Rinse under cold running water.
3. Place seafood in microproof baking dish with thick edges of fillets and steaks and thick ends of shellfish toward the outer edge of the dish.
4. Cover dish with plastic wrap or waxed paper.
5. Test often during the cooking period to avoid overcooking.
6. Method and time are the same for seafood with or without the shell.

COOKING GUIDE — SEAFOOD
Use COOK cycle.

Food	Time (minutes)	Standing Time (minutes)	Special Notes
Fish fillets, 1 lb. 2 lbs.	5½ - 7 9 - 10½	4 - 5 4 - 5	6 × 9 -inch dish, covered.
Fish steaks, 1 inch thick, 1 lb.	7 - 8	5 - 6	6 × 9 -inch dish, covered.
Whole fish 8 - 10 oz. 1½ - 2 lbs.	4 - 5½ 7 - 9	3 - 4 5	Appropriate shallow dish.
Crab legs 8 - 10 oz. 16 - 20 oz.	4 - 5½ 7 - 8	5 5	Appropriate shallow dish, covered. Turn once.
Shrimp, scallops 8 oz. 1 lb.	3 - 4½ 6 - 7½		Appropriate shallow dish, covered. Rearrange halfway.
Snails, clams, oysters, 12 oz.	3 - 4½		Shallow dish, covered. Rearrange halfway.
Lobster tails 1: 8 oz. 2: 8 oz. each 4: 8 oz. each	4 - 5½ 7 - 8 12 - 14	5 5 5	Shallow dish. Split shell to reduce curling.

COOKING/DEFROSTING GUIDE — CONVENIENCE SEAFOOD
Use COOK cycle.

Food	Amount	Time (minutes)	Special Notes
Shrimp croquettes	12 oz. package	7 - 9	Pierce sauce pouch, place on serving plate with croquettes. Cover, turn halfway through cooking time.
Fish sticks, frozen	4 oz. 8 oz.	2½ - 3 4 - 5½	Will not crisp. Cook on serving plate.
Tuna casserole, frozen	11 oz. package	5½ - 8	Remove from package to 1-quart casserole. Stir once during cooking and before serving.
Shrimp or crab newburg, frozen pouch	6½ oz.	5½ - 8	Place pouch on plate. Pierce pouch. Flex pouch to mix halfway through cooking time. Stir before serving.

Fish Fillets Amandine ———————— 4 servings
Total Cooking Time: 17 to 20 minutes

⅓ cup sliced or slivered
    almonds
¼ cup butter or margarine
1 pound fish fillets, cut
    in serving pieces
½ teaspoon salt
½ teaspoon lemon pepper

Place almonds and butter in 1½-quart round microproof baking dish. Use COOK cycle and cook 7 to 8 minutes, or until almonds are golden, stirring once during cooking time. Remove almonds with slotted spoon; set aside. Add fish fillets; turn to coat both sides. Cover with plastic wrap. Use COOK cycle and cook 10 to 12 minutes, or until fish flakes easily and is opaque. Sprinkle with salt, lemon pepper, and almonds. Cover and let stand 2 minutes before serving.

Poached Fish ———————— 4 servings
Total Cooking Time: 28 to 31 minutes

4 cups water
1 cup white wine
1 stalk celery with
    leaves, cut up
1 small onion, sliced
4 lemon slices
1½ teaspoons salt
5 peppercorns
    Fresh parsley
4 fish steaks (¾ to 1-inch
    thick), such as
    halibut or salmon

Combine all ingredients, except fish, in 2-quart microproof casserole. Cover. Use COOK cycle and cook 22 to 25 minutes, or until boiling. Strain liquid; return to casserole. Add fish; spoon liquid over top. Cover. Use COOK cycle and cook about 6 minutes (3 to 4 minutes per pound), or until fish flakes easily and is opaque. (To keep fish from becoming tough, do not overcook.) Let stand 3 minutes in liquid. Remove from liquid and place on serving platter.

Other liquids can be used for poaching, such as clam juice, chicken broth, or tomato juice.

Halibut and Vegetables —————— 2 servings
Total Cooking Time: 20 to 24 minutes

2 halibut steaks (6 to 8 ounces each) or similar fish
2 medium carrots, split lengthwise and in 2-inch strips
1 small onion, chopped
1 medium potato, peeled and cut in thin 2-inch strips
1 stalk celery, cut in thin 2-inch strips
½ green pepper, cut in thin 2-inch strips
1 small zucchini, cut in thin 2-inch strips
1 tablespoon minced fresh parsley
2 tablespoons butter or margarine
Salt
Freshly ground pepper
Paprika

Rinse fish steaks; pat dry with paper towels; set aside. Combine vegetables in shallow 1-quart microproof bowl. Dot with butter. Sprinkle with salt and pepper. Cover with plastic wrap. Use COOK cycle and cook 10 to 12 minutes, or until vegetables are almost tender; stir. Sprinkle with parsley. Arrange fish over vegetables, covering vegetables completely. Season lightly with salt, pepper, and paprika. Cover with plastic wrap. Use COOK cycle and cook 10 to 12 minutes, or until fish flakes easily and is opaque. Let stand, covered, 3 minutes before serving.

Tuna-Zucchini Medley ——————— 4 to 6 servings
Total Cooking Time: 24 to 29 minutes

1½ pounds zucchini, rinsed
  and sliced (about
  4 cups)
¼ cup water
1 can (7 ounces) tuna,
  drained and flaked
2 eggs, slightly beaten
1 cup fine bread crumbs,
  divided
1 teaspoon salt
½ teaspoon lemon pepper
2 tablespoons butter or
  margarine

Place zucchini in 2-quart microproof casserole. Add water. Cover. Use COOK cycle and cook 10 to 12 minutes, or until crisp-tender, stirring once during cooking time. Drain. Add tuna, eggs, ½ cup of the bread crumbs, salt, and lemon pepper; mix carefully; set aside.

In 1-cup glass measure, combine butter and remaining ½ cup bread crumbs. Use DEFROST cycle and cook 2 minutes; stir. Sprinkle crumbs over casserole. Use COOK cycle and cook 12 to 15 minutes, or until center is set, rotating once during cooking. Let stand, covered, 5 minutes before serving.

Lemon-Buttered Cod Fillets ——————— 4 servings
Total Cooking Time: 10 to 12 minutes

1 pound cod fillets
2 tablespoons butter or
  margarine
2 tablespoons lemon juice
½ teaspoon lemon pepper
½ teaspoon salt
  Paprika

Arrange fillets in shallow 1½-quart oval microproof casserole or glass pie plate. Dot with butter. Sprinkle with remaining ingredients. Cover with plastic wrap. Use COOK cycle and cook 10 to 12 minutes, or until fish flakes easily and is opaque. Let stand 2 minutes before serving.

Salmon Ring —————————— 6 to 8 servings

Total Cooking Time: 10 to 12 minutes

1 can (1 pound) red salmon,
   undrained
2 eggs, beaten
1 cup fresh bread crumbs
¼ cup chopped dill pickle
3 tablespoons minced green
   onion
2 tablespoons mayonnaise
¼ teaspoon salt
⅛ teaspoon freshly ground
   pepper
Parslied Potatoes (page 74)
Minced fresh parsley

Grease 4-cup microproof ring mold. In large bowl, combine all ingredients, except potatoes and parsley; blend well. Turn into prepared mold, spreading evenly. Cover. Use COOK cycle and cook 10 to 12 minutes. Invert onto serving platter.

   Fill center of ring with potatoes. Sprinkle with parsley.

Use your imagination in choosing other fillings for this attractive ring. Broccoli, creamed peas and carrots, pearl onions, Brussels sprouts, or rice are our suggestions. You might also simply serve this Salmon Ring with White Sauce (page 73).

Salmon Ring, Broccoli and Sour Cream (page 73), Parslied Potatoes (page 74) →

Salmon Steak with Cucumber Sauce

2 servings

Total Cooking Time: 7 to 8 minutes

¼ cup finely chopped, peeled and seeded cucumber
2 tablespoons mayonnaise
2 tablespoons dairy sour cream
½ teaspoon chopped chives or ¼ teaspoon freeze-dried chives
½ teaspoon onion flakes
⅛ teaspoon salt
2 salmon steaks (1-inch thick)
Lemon pepper

In small bowl, combine cucumber, mayonnaise, sour cream, chives, onion flakes, and salt; set aside.

Place salmon in 2 microproof au gratin dishes or 1 8-inch microproof pie plate. Sprinkle with lemon pepper. Cover with plastic wrap. Use COOK cycle and cook 5 to 6 minutes, or until fish flakes easily and is opaque. Drain, if necessary.

Spoon cucumber sauce over salmon. Use DEFROST cycle and cook 2 minutes, or until sauce is warm. Let stand 2 minutes before serving.

To prepare 4 salmon steaks, prepare cucumber sauce, doubling ingredients. Arrange salmon steaks in 10-inch round microproof dish with narrow ends in center. Use COOK cycle and cook 9 to 12 minutes. Spoon Cucumber Sauce over salmon. Use DEFROST cycle and cook 4 to 6 minutes, or until sauce is warm.

To reduce calories, omit the sauce and serve with lemon wedges and minced fresh parsley.

Hawaiian Baked Fish ———————— 4 to 6 servings
Total Cooking Time: 12 to 14 minutes

1 cup pineapple juice
2 tablespoons lemon juice
2 tablespoons butter or
   margarine
1 tablespoon minced pimiento
1 tablespoon instant minced
   onion
1½ teaspoons cornstarch
1 teaspoon parsley flakes
½ teaspoon curry powder
2 cups cooked rice
1 pound fresh or thawed
   frozen fish fillets

In 2-cup glass measure, combine pineapple juice, lemon juice, butter, pimiento, onion, cornstarch, parsley, and curry powder; blend well. Use COOK cycle and cook 5 to 6 minutes, or until mixture begins to thicken, stirring twice during cooking.

Spread rice in shallow 1½-quart microproof casserole. Roll up fillets and place on top of rice. Pour sauce over all. Cover with plastic wrap. Use COOK cycle and cook 7 to 8 minutes, or until fish flakes easily and is opaque. Let stand, covered, 3 minutes, before serving. Garnish with pineapple, if desired.

Herb-Crumbed Fish Fillets ——————— 4 servings
Total Cooking Time: 6 to 7 minutes

4 fish fillets (½ pound)
⅓ cup seasoned Italian
   bread crumbs
¼ cup grated Parmesan cheese
¼ teaspoon garlic powder
¼ teaspoon salt
1 egg white, slightly
   beaten

Rinse fillets; pat dry with paper towels; set aside. In small bowl, combine crumbs, cheese, garlic powder, and salt. Dip fillets in egg white, then in crumb mixture; coat well. Arrange fillets in shallow microproof baking dish, placing thickest part of fillet toward outside of dish. Cover with paper towel. Use COOK cycle and cook 6 to 7 minutes, or until fish flakes easily. Let stand 2 minutes. Serve with lemon wedges.

Poor Man's Lobster ———————— 4 servings
Total Cooking Time: 16 to 17 minutes

1 pound cod, boned and cut
   in bite-size pieces
2 cups water
2 tablespoons onion flakes
1 stalk celery, sliced
1 bay leaf
½ teaspoon salt
4 peppercorns
1 cup butter or margarine
¼ cup lemon juice

Combine all ingredients, except butter and lemon juice, in 2-quart microproof bowl. Use COOK cycle and cook 14 to 15 minutes, or until fish flakes easily and is opaque, stirring once during cooking. Let stand 5 minutes. While fish is standing, combine butter and lemon juice in 2-cup glass measure. Use COOK cycle and cook 2 minutes. Remove cod from cooking broth with a slotted spoon; place on serving platter. Serve with lemon butter for dipping.

←Herb-Crumbed Fish Fillets

Baked Stuffed Fish Fillets ——————— 6 servings
Total Cooking Time: 12 to 13 minutes

2 tablespoons butter or
   margarine
2 tablespoons minced green
   onion
1/2 cup bread crumbs
2/3 cup chopped mushrooms
2 pounds flounder or
   sole fillets
   White Sauce (page 73)
1/4 cup white wine
1/2 cup shredded Swiss
   cheese
1 teaspoon chopped fresh
   parsley
1/2 teaspoon paprika

Combine butter, onion, and mushrooms in 4-cup glass measure. Use COOK cycle and cook 3 minutes, or until onion is transparent; mix in bread crumbs. Rinse and pat dry fillets. Divide crumb mixture onto each fillet. Roll fillets; place, seam-side down, in 6 × 9-inch microproof baking dish; set aside. Prepare white sauce. When thick and hot, stir in cheese until melted. Stir in wine and pour over fish. Cover with plastic wrap. Use COOK cycle and cook 9 to 10 minutes, or until fish is opaque. Sprinkle with parsley and paprika. Serve hot.

Clams with Creamy
Garlic Sauce ————————————— 4 servings
Total Cooking Time: 15½ to 18 minutes

24 clams in the shell,
   well scrubbed

Sauce

2 tablespoons onion, finely
   minced
1 clove garlic, finely minced
2 tablespoons dry white wine
1/4 teaspoon salt
1/8 teaspoon pepper
1/2 cup butter, chilled and
   cut into 8 pieces

Arrange half the clams in a circle on a microproof plate with hinges toward rim. Use COOK cycle and cook 3 to 4 minutes, or until shells open. Remove as soon as they open. Repeat with remaining shells. Break off top shell and arrange in a circle on plate. Cover with plastic wrap. Set aside.

In a 4-cup glass measure, combine onion, garlic, wine, salt, and pepper. Use COOK cycle and cook 3½ minutes. Quickly whisk in butter, 1 tablespoon at a time. Return to oven. Use COOK cycle and cook for 30 second intervals after 2 tablespoons butter are added. The sauce should be creamy and slightly thickened. Spoon butter sauce on each clam. Serve hot.

Poached Oysters ———————————— 4 to 6 servings
Total Cooking Time: 4 to 6 minutes

2 tablespoons butter
2 tablespoons flour
1/8 teaspoon white pepper
1 pint oysters, drained,
reserve liquid
1 cup oyster liquid and milk
to equal 1 cup
1/2 teaspoon Worcestershire
sauce
1/2 teaspoon lemon juice
Buttered toast tips
Paprika or cayenne pepper
Minced fresh parsley

Place butter in 4-cup glass measure. Use COOK cycle and cook 1 minute, or until butter is melted. Stir in flour. Use COOK cycle and cook 1·minute. Briskly stir in oyster liquid and milk mixture. Use COOK cycle and cook 5 to 6 minutes, or until thickened. Stir in oysters, Worcestershire and lemon juice. Use DEFROST cycle and cook 2 to 3 minutes, stirring once. Serve on toast tips. Sprinkle with paprika and parsley.

Shrimp Newburg ———————————— 4 servings
Total Cooking Time: 20 to 24 minutes

1/4 cup butter or margarine
1/4 cup chopped onion
2 tablespoons all-purpose
flour
1/2 teaspoon salt
1 1/2 cups milk
2 egg yolks, beaten
1 teaspoon grated lemon
rind
1 package (8 to 12 ounces)
frozen cooked shrimp,
thawed
1 can (4 ounces) sliced
mushrooms, drained

Combine butter and onion in 2-quart microproof casserole. Use COOK cycle and cook 3 to 4 minutes, or until onion is transparent. Stir in flour and salt. Use COOK cycle and cook 1 minute. Pour milk into 2-cup glass measure. Use COOK cycle and cook 3 minutes, or until warm. Stir into flour mixture; blend until smooth. Use COOK cycle and cook 4 to 5 minutes, stirring once during cooking time. Stir small amount into egg yolks; then pour egg mixture back into sauce; blend well. Stir in lemon rind. Use DEFROST cycle and cook 5 minutes, or until thickened and hot, stirring every 2 minutes. Stir in shrimp and mushrooms. Use DEFROST cycle and cook 4 to 6 minutes. Serve over rice or toast points.

To substitute fresh mushrooms for canned, combine with onion and butter. Use COOK cycle and cook 6 to 8 minutes.

Jambalaya ———————————— 4 servings
Total Cooking Time: 10 minutes

2 slices bacon, cut into
   pieces
1 can (10¾ ounces)
   tomato purée
1 can (4½ ounces) large
   shrimp, drained
1 cup water
1 cup quick-cooking rice
1 teaspoon onion flakes
1 teaspoon parsley flakes
½ teaspoon Worcestershire
   sauce
¼ teaspoon thyme

Place bacon in 2-quart microproof casserole. Use COOK cycle and cook 2 minutes; drain. Add remaining ingredients; stir to blend. Use COOK cycle and cook 8 minutes, or until rice is tender. Let stand 3 minutes before serving.

HOME BAKED GOODNESS

Cakes cooked in the microwave oven are checked for doneness with the classic toothpick test (right). Custard cups, arranged in a circle, cook muffins (above).

Treat your family and friends to the rich aroma of a hot-from-the-oven homemade bread. For a quick and easy surprise breakfast, or as a coffee-klatch companion, you can count on baked goods from the microwave oven.

All baked goods have excellent texture, but they do not brown or develop crust. There is no hot air to dry the surface as in conventional baking. For this reason, most microwave recipes call for dark flours, or add molasses and spices. The ab-

sent crust is a benefit, however, enabling much higher rising of cakes and bread. For this reason, larger loaf pans are often recommended. It's also beneficial to use ring molds or bundt-type microproof pans for more even cooking.

Are there any chocolate-covered-cherries fans at your house? If so, you'll want to start off with Chocolate Cherry Bundt Cake (page 152). Pecan Rum Pie (page 150), too, is a can't-wait-to-try treat.

Converting Your Recipes

When adapting "quick bread" recipes, you will find it necessary to reduce the amount of leavening (baking powder or soda) by about one-quarter the normal amount. A bitter aftertaste is apparent if too much leavening is used in biscuits or muffins. Since food rises higher in the microwave oven, you will not see a loss in volume from the reduction of soda or baking powder. If a recipe contains buttermilk or sour cream, do not change the amount of soda, since it serves to counteract the sour taste and does not act only as a leavening agent. When using a mix where leavening cannot be reduced, if you allow the dough to stand about 10 minutes before cooking, some of the gas will be lost. And observe the following tips:

☐ Fill paper-lined muffin cups only half full to allow for muffins rising more.
☐ You can prepare your own "brown 'n serve" breads and rolls by baking them ahead in the microwave oven. Then place them in the conventional oven to brown just before serving.
☐ Breads and rolls should be reheated to the point where they are warm to the touch. Overheating or overcooking makes bread tough and rubbery.
☐ When making yeast bread in a microwave oven, choose a recipe with cornmeal, whole wheat flour, or rye flour to achieve a rich color.

COOKING GUIDE — PUDDING AND PIE FILLING MIX

Food	Amount	Time (minutes)	Control	Special Notes
Pudding and pie filling mix	3¼ ounces 5½ ounces	7½ - 9 11 - 13	COOK COOK	Follow package directions. Stir every 3 minutes. Use 4-cup glass measure.
Egg custard	3 ounces	8½ - 11	COOK	Follow package directions. Stir every 3 minutes. Use 4-cup glass measure.
Tapioca	3¼ ounces	7 - 9	COOK	Follow package directions. Stir every 3 minutes. Use 4-cup glass measure.

COOKING/WARMING/DEFROSTING GUIDE — CONVENIENCE BREADS

Food	Amount	Control	Time	Special Notes
Hamburger buns, hot dog rolls, frozen	1 lb.	DEFROST	3½ - 4½ minutes	Use original microproof container, paper plate, or towels. Place on microproof rack, turn over after 2 minutes.
Room temperature:	1	COOK	10 - 15 seconds	
	2	COOK	15 - 20 seconds	
	4	COOK	20 - 25 seconds	
	6	COOK	25 - 30 seconds	
Doughnuts, sweet rolls, muffins	1	COOK	15 - 20 seconds	Place on paper plate or towel. Add 15 seconds if frozen.
	2	COOK	25 - 30 seconds	
	4	COOK	40 - 50 seconds	
	6	COOK	50 - 60 seconds	
Whole coffee cake, frozen	10 - 13 oz.	COOK	2 - 2½ minutes	Place on paper plate or towel.
Room temperature:	10 - 13 oz.	COOK	1¼ - 1¾ minutes	Place on paper plate or towel.
French bread, frozen	1 lb.	COOK	2 - 2¾ minutes	Place on paper plate or towel.
Room temperature:	1 lb.	COOK	25 - 35 seconds	
English muffins, waffles, frozen	2	COOK	45 - 60 seconds	Place on paper towels. Toast in toaster after defrosting, if desired.
Corn bread mix	15 oz.	COOK	15 - 16½ minutes	Use 9" round dish, paper-lined custard cups, or microproof muffin tray. Turn dish if rising unevenly. Let stand 5 minutes before serving.
Nut bread mix	6 muffins	COOK	3 - 4 minutes	Let stand 2 minutes before serving.
	15 - 17 oz.	COOK	20 minutes	Use 1½-quart bowl with glass in center. Let stand 5 minutes before serving.
Blueberry muffin mix	4	COOK	1½ - 2¼ minutes	Use paper-lined custard cups or microproof muffin tray. Let stand 2 minutes before serving.
	6	COOK	3 - 4 minutes	
Bread, frozen	1 slice	DEFROST	15 - 20 seconds	Place on paper plate or towels. Let stand 5 minutes before serving.
	1 lb. loaf	DEFROST	2 - 3 minutes	In original plastic bag, remove twister. Let stand 5 minutes before serving.
Coffeecake mix	19 oz.	COOK	17½ - 19 minutes	Use 9" round dish. Turn dish if rising unevenly. Let stand 5 minutes before serving.

Holiday Bread Ring ―――――――― 10 to 12 servings
Total Cooking Time: 13 to 14 minutes

¾ cup milk
½ cup butter or margarine
2¼ to 3 cups all-purpose flour
¼ cup sugar
1 egg
1 package active dry
 yeast
1 teaspoon salt
1 teaspoon cardamom seed
½ cup raisins
¼ cup chopped nuts
¼ cup chopped candied red
 cherries
1 tablespoon grated fresh
 orange peel
2 tablespoons sugar
1 teaspoon cinnamon
¼ cup sliced almonds

In 2-cup glass measure, combine milk and butter. Use COOK cycle and cook 2 minutes, or until warm (120°F on microproof thermometer). Stir to melt butter.

In large mixing bowl, combine 2 cups flour, sugar, egg, yeast, salt, cardamom, and warm milk mixture. Mix with electric mixer 3 to 4 minutes. Stir in raisins, chopped nuts, cherries, and orange peel. Stir in enough flour to form soft dough.

Generously grease 12-cup microproof bundt-type pan. Combine sugar and cinnamon. Sprinkle inside of prepared pan, shaking to coat all sides; use all mixture. Sprinkle almonds in bottom. Spoon batter into pan; spread evenly. Cover with plastic wrap. Fill a tall, thin glass with 1 cup water. Place pan and water in oven. Use DEFROST cycle and cook 2 minutes. Let stand 1 hour in oven.

When dough has doubled, remove plastic wrap and glass of water. Use COOK cycle and cook 9 to 10 minutes, or until bread springs back when lightly touched. Rotate dish, if bread is cooking unevenly. Let stand 10 minutes. Invert onto serving plate; cool before serving.

Pumpkin Cupcakes (page 150), Holiday Bread Ring→

Pumpkin Cupcakes _____ 12 servings
Total Cooking Time: 11 to 12 minutes

1 egg
½ cup firmly packed brown
   sugar
¼ cup sugar
6 tablespoons vegetable oil
½ cup canned or cooked
   mashed pumpkin
½ teaspoon vanilla
1 cup all-purpose flour
2 tablespoons milk
½ teaspoon cinnamon
½ teaspoon salt
¼ teaspoon baking powder
¼ teaspoon baking soda
⅛ teaspoon ginger
   Cream Cheese Frosting
   (page 154)

In mixing bowl, beat egg, sugars, and oil until smooth. Blend in pumpkin and vanilla. Add remaining ingredients, except frosting; stir until smooth. Line 6 cups in microproof cupcake pan or 6 glass custard cups with paper liners. Fill ½ full with batter. Use DEFROST cycle and cook 5½ to 6 minutes, or until cupcakes test done, rotating cups if rising unevenly. Repeat with remaining batter. Cool and frost with Cream Cheese Frosting.

Pecan Rum Pie _____ 6 to 8 servings
Total Cooking Time: 13 to 14 minutes

¼ cup butter or margarine
1½ cups pecan halves
1 cup sugar
½ cup dark corn syrup
3 eggs, slightly beaten
1 teaspoon rum flavoring or
   vanilla extract
1 baked (9-inch) pie shell
   in microproof dish

Place butter in 2-quart glass measure or bowl. Use COOK cycle and cook 1 minute, or until melted. Blend in nuts, sugar, corn syrup, eggs, and rum. Pour into pie shell. Use COOK cycle and cook 12 to 13 minutes, or until center is set. Cool to room temperature before serving.

Cheesecake and Raspberry Sauce —————— 6 to 8 servings

Total Cooking Time: 8 to 10 minutes

¾ cup graham cracker crumbs
¾ cup sugar, divided
3 tablespoons butter or margarine
2 tablespoons firmly packed brown sugar
1 teaspoon cinnamon
1 package (8 ounces) cream cheese, quartered
2 eggs
1 teaspoon vanilla
1 cup dairy sour cream
Raspberry Sauce (page 171)

Combine crumbs, 2 tablespoons of sugar, butter, brown sugar, and cinnamon in 8-inch round microproof cake dish. Use COOK cycle and cook 1½ minutes. Stir to combine. Press crumbs evenly over bottom and sides of cake dish.

Place cream cheese in small microproof bowl. Use DEFROST cycle and cook 30 seconds, or until softened. Gradually beat in ½ cup of sugar until dissolved. Add eggs and vanilla; mix well. Pour into prepared crust. Use COOK cycle and cook 5 to 6 minutes, or until nearly set in center, rotating dish if cake is cooking unevenly.

In small bowl, combine sour cream and remaining 2 tablespoons sugar; blend well. Spread carefully and evenly over filling. Use COOK cycle and cook 1½ to 2 minutes, rotating after 1 minute. Edges should be set and center still soft. Cool to room temperature. Refrigerate at least 12 hours. Pass Raspberry Sauce with sliced cheesecake.

Cheesecake can be topped with any fruit in season, such as blueberries, strawberries, or peaches.

Chocolate Cherry Bundt Cake — 10 to 12 servings

Total Cooking Time: 18 to 20 minutes

1 tablespoon sugar
1 package (18½ ounces)
  chocolate cake mix
  with pudding
1 cup cherry pie filling
3 eggs
¾ cup water
¼ cup vegetable oil
1 teaspoon almond extract
  White Cap Glaze (below)

Generously grease 12-cup microproof bundt-type pan; chill. Sprinkle with 1 tablespoon sugar; shake well to coat. Mix remaining ingredients, except glaze, following cake package directions. Pour carefully into prepared pan. Use COOK cycle and cook 18 to 20 minutes, or until cake tests done, rotating one-quarter turn at 5 minute intervals. Let stand 10 minutes before inverting onto serving plate to cool. Drizzle White Cap Glaze over cake. Let stand until glaze sets. Serve.

For an extra festive treat, top cake with additional cherries from remaining pie filling.

White Cap Glaze —————————— ½ cup

Total Cooking Time: 30 seconds

1 package (3 ounces) cream
  cheese
¾ cup confectioners sugar
3 to 4 teaspoons milk

Remove foil from cream cheese. Place in 1-quart microproof bowl. Use DEFROST cycle and cook 30 seconds, or until softened. Beat in sugar and milk until smooth.

Chocolate Cherry Bundt Cake→

Raisin-Oatmeal Muffins ⎯⎯⎯⎯⎯⎯ 18 servings
Total Cooking Time: 16 to 18 minutes

1 cup all-purpose flour
⅔ cup quick-cooking oatmeal
¼ cup firmly packed brown
    sugar
1 teaspoon baking powder
½ teaspoon baking soda
½ teaspoon salt
1½ teaspoons cinnamon,
    divided
2 eggs
½ cup vegetable oil
½ cup buttermilk
½ cup raisins
2 tablespoons sugar

In small mixing bowl, combine flour, oatmeal, brown sugar, baking powder, baking soda, salt, and ½ teaspoon cinnamon. Add eggs, oil, buttermilk, and raisins. Stir until just moistened. Spoon batter into 6 paper-lined custard cups or microproof muffin pan, filling each about half full. Mix remaining cinnamon and sugar. Sprinkle top of each muffin with about ¼ teaspoon sugar-cinnamon mixture. Place 6 custard cups in a circle in oven. Use COOK cycle and cook 5½ to 6 minutes, rotating cups or pan if muffins are rising unevenly. Repeat with remaining batter. Serve warm.

Cream Cheese Frosting ⎯⎯⎯⎯⎯⎯ 1½ cups
Total Cooking Time: ½ to 1 minute

1 package (3 ounces) cream
    cheese
2 tablespoons butter or
    margarine
2 cups confectioners sugar
½ teaspoon vanilla
1 to 2 teaspoons milk

In 1-quart microproof bowl, combine cream cheese and butter. Use COOK cycle and cook ½ to 1 minute, or until softened. Beat in sugar, vanilla, and enough milk for spreading consistency.

Butter Pecan
Ice Cream Pie _____ 6 to 8 servings

Total Cooking Time: 3½ to 4 minutes

6 tablespoons butter or
   margarine
¾ cup all-purpose flour
¾ cup finely ground pecans,
   divided
3 tablespoons firmly packed
   brown sugar
1 quart butter pecan
   ice cream

Place butter in 4-cup glass measure. Use COOK cycle and cook 1½ minutes, or until melted. Stir in flour, half of the pecans, and sugar; mix well. Press mixture firmly onto bottom and sides of 9-inch microproof pie plate. Use COOK cycle and cook 2½ minutes, rotating after 1 minute. Cool to room temperature. Spoon ice cream into shell. (If ice cream is very firm, place carton on microproof plate. Use DEFROST cycle and cook 1 to 2 minutes, or until softened.) Sprinkle remaining pecans over top. Freeze until firm.

Granola Crunch Cake _____ 12 servings

Total Cooking Time: 18 to 20 minutes

1 tablespoon sugar
1½ cups granola, divided
1 package (18½ ounces)
   yellow cake mix
1 package (3⅝ ounces)
   instant butterscotch
   pudding
3 eggs
¾ cup water
¼ cup vegetable oil

Generously grease 12-cup fluted microproof bundt-type pan; chill. Sprinkle inside with sugar; shake to coat all sides. Sprinkle ¼ cup of the granola into prepared pan.
   In large mixing bowl, combine cake and pudding mixes, eggs, water, and oil. Mix according to cake package directions. Carefully pour three-fourths of the batter over granola in prepared pan. Sprinkle remaining granola over batter. Use COOK cycle and cook 18 to 20 minutes, or until cake tests done, rotating one-quarter turn every 5 minutes. Let stand 10 minutes. Invert onto serving plate. Cool before slicing.

Upside-Down Apple Cake ———— 1 8-inch cake
Total Cooking Time: 19½ to 20½ minutes

1 cooking apple
¼ cup butter or margarine
⅓ cup honey
⅓ cup chopped nuts
¼ cup chopped maraschino
   cherries
1¼ cups all-purpose flour
¾ cup sugar
½ cup milk
⅓ cup shortening
1 egg
1½ teaspoons baking powder
1 teaspoon vanilla
½ teaspoon salt

Core unpeeled apple. Slice into ⅛-inch thick rings; cover and set aside.
   Place butter in 9-inch microproof cake dish. Use COOK cycle and cook 1½ minutes, or until melted. Stir in honey. Add apple rings. Use COOK cycle and cook 4 minutes, turning apple rings after 2 minutes. Sprinkle with nuts and cherries; set aside.
   In small mixing bowl, combine flour, sugar, milk, shortening, egg, baking powder, vanilla, and salt. Beat 3 minutes, scraping bowl once. Carefully spoon batter over apple rings in cake dish. Use COOK cycle and cook 14 to 15 minutes, or until cake tests done, rotating dish if cake is rising unevenly. Invert onto serving plate. Let cake stand in dish 3 to 4 minutes. Remove dish and let cake stand 10 minutes. Serve warm.

Pumpkin Walnut Bread ———————— 1 loaf
Total Cooking Time: 20 to 24 minutes

2 tablespoons graham
   cracker crumbs
¾ cup firmly packed brown
   sugar
½ cup vegetable oil
2 eggs
2 tablespoons milk
1 cup canned or cooked
   mashed pumpkin
1 cup all-purpose flour
¾ cup chopped walnuts
⅛ teaspoon cinnamon
¾ teaspoon salt
½ teaspoon nutmeg
½ teaspoon baking powder
½ teaspoon baking soda

Grease bottom and sides of 8 × 4-inch microproof loaf dish. Sprinkle with graham cracker crumbs. Shake out excess; set aside.
   In large mixing bowl, blend sugar and oil. Beat in eggs, milk, and pumpkin. Add remaining ingredients; mix well. Pour batter into prepared dish; spread evenly. Use COOK cycle and cook 20 to 24 minutes, or until bread tests done in center, rotating loaf during cooking time, if bread is rising unevenly. Let stand 10 minutes in dish. Remove from dish and let stand to cool completely. To develop flavor, wrap in foil and chill several hours before slicing. Serve with butter or cream cheese.

Maple Nut Ring —————————— 6 servings
Total Cooking Time: 4 to 4½ minutes

2 tablespoons butter or
    margarine
¼ cup firmly packed brown
    sugar
2 tablespoons chopped nuts
1 tablespoon maple syrup
1 teaspoon maple extract
1 can (10 ounces)
    refrigerator biscuits

Place butter in 8-inch microproof pie plate. Use COOK cycle and cook 30 seconds, or until melted. Add sugar, nuts, syrup and extract; blend well. Separate biscuit dough into 10 pieces. Arrange each piece in pie plate, slightly overlapping, to form a ring. Press biscuits gently together, leaving an opening in the center. Place glass custard cup in center. Use COOK cycle and cook 3½ to 4 minutes, or until rolls spring back when lightly touched.

Remove custard cup. Invert onto serving plate. Syrup will run over bread ring. Remove pie plate. Let stand 3 minutes before serving.

Classic Coconut Cake ——————— 10 to 12 servings
Total Cooking Time: 13 to 14½ minutes

1 package (18½ ounces)
    white cake mix
½ cup shredded coconut,
    finely chopped
1½ teaspoons grated lemon
    peel
Frosting
1 cup sugar
½ cup water
¼ teaspoon cream of tartar
    Dash of salt
2 egg whites
1 teaspoon vanilla
1 cup shredded coconut

Prepare cake mix according to package directions. Fold in ½ cup coconut and lemon peel. Pour half of batter into 9 inch microproof cake pan. Use COOK cycle and cook 7½ to 8½ minutes, or until cake tests done. Let stand 5 minutes on flat, heat resistant surface. Transfer to wire rack; let cool. Repeat with remaining batter.

To prepare Frosting, combine sugar, water, cream of tartar, and salt in a 2-cup glass measure. Use COOK cycle and cook 5½ minutes. In a small mixing bowl, beat egg whites with an electric mixer until soft peaks form. Gradually add hot syrup mixture to egg whites, beating continuously. Continue beating 5 minutes, or until mixture is thick and fluffy. While beating, add vanilla. Frost cake and sprinkle with coconut on top and sides.

Brown & Serve Rolls ——————————— 12 rolls

Total Cooking Time: 22 to 24 minutes

1 loaf (1 pound) frozen
    bread dough

Place frozen dough on lightly greased 9-inch pie plate. Fill a 1-cup glass measure with water. Use COOK cycle and cook 3½ to 4 minutes, or until water boils. Move water to rear of unit, cover dough with a damp cloth. Place in oven. Use DEFROST cycle and cook 4 minutes; turn loaf over. Use DEFROST cycle and cook 4 minutes. Dough may now be worked and shaped. Form into twelve rolls or eighteen ¾-inch balls. Grease microproof muffin pan. Place three ¾-inch balls into each muffin cup. Set dough aside in a warm draft free area until it doubles in size. When doubled, use COOK cycle and cook 4 to 6 minutes, rotating dish twice. When rolls are done, the center should spring back when lightly touched. Freeze or refrigerate until ready to brown.

Before baking, rolls may be brushed with butter and coated with crushed dry onion flakes or buttered bread crumbs, poppy or sesame seeds. For an added touch before browning in the toaster oven or conventional oven, brush with beaten egg wash to give a professional bakery gloss.

Rice Pie Crust ——————————— 1 9-inch pie shell

Total Cooking Time: 1½ to 2 minutes

1½ cups cooked rice
1 egg, slightly beaten
⅓ cup shredded Cheddar
    cheese
1 tablespoon parsley flakes

In mixing bowl, combine all ingredients; mix well. Press evenly over bottom and sides of 9-inch glass pie plate. Use COOK cycle and cook 1½ to 2 minutes, or until cheese is melted.

This crust is naturally low in calories. It can be used with many different fillings and is especially nice as the base for Onion Pie in Rice Crust (page 75).

Savory Cheese Bread _____ 2 loaves
Total Cooking Time: 21 to 23 minutes

1 cup milk
½ cup butter or margarine
2¾ cups all-purpose flour
2 tablespoons sugar
½ teaspoon salt
1 package (1 ounce) active
   dry yeast
1 egg
1 envelope onion soup mix,
   divided
1 cup shredded Cheddar
   cheese, divided

In 2-cup glass measure, combine milk and butter. Use COOK cycle and cook 3 minutes, or to 120°F on microproof thermometer.

In large mixing bowl, mix flour, sugar, salt, and yeast. Add milk mixture and egg. In small bowl, mix 2 tablespoons of soup mix and ¼ cup of cheese; set aside. Add remaining soup mix and cheese to batter.

Divide batter evenly between 2 well greased 8 × 4 × 3-inch microproof loaf pans. Sprinkle with reserved onion-cheese mixture. Cover lightly. Let rise in warm place, free from draft, 1 to 1½ hours, or until double in volume. Cook 1 loaf at a time. Use COOK cycle and cook 9 to 10 minutes, or until bread springs back when lightly touched, sides recede from pan, and top is no longer moist. Turn out of pans and cool on wire rack.

Garlic Bread _____ 12 servings
Total Cooking Time: 2 to 2½ minutes

1 loaf (16 ounces) French,
   Italian, or sourdough
   bread
½ cup butter or margarine,
   softened
2 cloves garlic, minced or
   1 teaspoon garlic
   powder
½ cup grated Parmesan or
   Romano cheese
   Paprika

Cut loaf in 1-inch thick slices without cutting through bottom crust. In small bowl, blend butter and garlic. Spread on bread slices; then sprinkle with cheese and paprika. Place loaf on paper towel-lined microproof plate. Use COOK cycle and cook 2 to 2½ minutes, or until heated through.

Onion Herb Bread ———————————— 12 servings

Total Cooking Time: 2 to 2½ minutes

1 loaf (16 ounces) French,
   Italian, or sourdough
   bread
½ cup butter or margarine,
   softened
1 tablespoon instant onion
   flakes
1 tablespoon snipped parsley
½ teaspoon dillweed
¼ teaspoon onion salt
   Paprika

Cut loaf in 1-inch thick slices without cutting through bottom crust. In small bowl, blend remaining ingredients, except paprika. Spread on bread slices. Sprinkle with paprika. Place loaf on paper towel-lined microproof plate. Use COOK cycle and cook 2 to 2½ minutes, or until heated through.

SPECIAL TREATS

Carefully select the microproof cookware for bar cookies (left). If you don't have a microproof candy thermometer, check with conventional, outside the oven (above).

If you're like many cooks, candy has been one of those items yet to achieve homemade status with you. That's about to change and you'll never regret it! The fuss and mess of double boilers has been eliminated by the microwave oven. It's truly so easy that you'll soon laugh to yourself as friends are amazed by your talent.

You'll also soon be churning out an array of bar cookies that will have a line of neighborhood kids at your kitchen door. Raisin-

Nut Bars (page 167) and Lemon Bars (page 168) were the favorites of the test kitchen but be sure to try your own recipes, too, and others here.

Fruit specialties and sauces are also excellent and easier than — well, everything *is* easy in the microwave, isn't it?

We hope you've enjoyed this book and, more importantly, are convinced that the world of microwave cooking is a special treat of its own. Good fortune and good cooking to you!

Converting Your Recipes

To make candy, simply find a similar recipe here. You'll be trying all those recipes you've been longing to do. For other desserts, consult these tips as well as similar recipes:

- ☐ You can enhance your light batter cookies and cakes with cinnamon, nutmeg, brown sugar, coffee, nuts, toppings, frostings, glazes, food coloring, etc.
- ☐ Small drop cookies and slice 'n bake cookies don't do as well as the larger bar cookies. Drop cookies must be cooked in small batches; they tend to cook unevenly, and need to be removed individually from the oven when finished.
- ☐ A serviceable cookie sheet can be made by covering cardboard with waxed paper.
- ☐ For even cooking, select fruit of uniform size to be cooked whole, as in baked apples, or to be cooked in pieces, as in apple pie.
- ☐ Stirring sauces quickly two or three times during cooking is sufficient to ensure even cooking. Too may stirrings may slow cooking.

COOKING/DEFROSTING GUIDE — CONVENIENCE DESSERTS

Food	Amount	Control	Time	Special Notes
Brownies, other bars, frozen	12 - 13 oz.	DEFROST	2 - 3 minutes	In original ¾" foil tray, lid removed. Let stand 5 minutes.
Cookies, frozen	6	DEFROST	50 - 60 seconds	Place on paper plate or towels.
Pineapple upside-down cake mix	21½ oz.	COOK	8½ minutes	Use 9" round glass dish. Remove enough batter for 2 cupcakes, bake separately. Rotate if rising unevenly.
Cupcakes or crumb cakes, frozen	1 or 2	DEFROST	½ - 1 minute	Place on shallow plate.
Cheesecake, frozen	17 - 19 oz.	DEFROST	4 - 5 minutes	Remove from foil pan to plate. Let stand 1 minute.
Pound cake, frozen	10¾ oz.	DEFROST	2 minutes	Remove from foil pan to plate. Rotate once. Let stand 5 minutes.
Cake, frozen 2- or 3-layer	17 oz.	DEFROST	2½ - 3 minutes	Remove from foil pan to plate. Watch carefully, frosting melts fast. Let stand 5 minutes.
Custard pie, frozen	9" pie	COOK	5 - 6 minutes	Remove from foil pan to plate. Center should be nearly set.
Fruit pie, frozen, unbaked, 2 crusts	9" pie	COOK	17½ - 20 minutes	On glass pie plate. Brown, if desired, in preheated 425° conventional oven 8 - 10 minutes.
Frozen fruit	10 oz.	COOK	6½ - 7½ minutes	On microproof plate. Slit pouch. Flex halfway through cooking time to mix.
	16 oz.	COOK	9 - 11 minutes	Remove from bag. Place in glass casserole, cover. Stir halfway through cooking time.
Cake mix	18½ oz.	COOK	16 minutes	Follow package directions. 12-cup bundt-type pan. Rotate every 5 minutes.

Chocolate Fudge _____ 3 pounds

Total Cooking Time: 13 to 15 minutes

3 cups sugar
½ cup butter or margarine
1 can (5⅓ ounces)
   evaporated milk
2 cups (12 ounces) semisweet
   chocolate pieces
1 jar (7 ounces) marshmallow
   creme
1 cup chopped nuts
1 teaspoon vanilla

Lightly butter a 13×9-inch baking pan. Combine sugar, butter, and milk in 3-quart glass bowl. Use COOK cycle and cook 13 to 15 minutes, or until a small amount dropped in cold water forms a soft ball (234°F on microproof candy thermometer). Stir in chocolate pieces and marshmallow creme until mixture is thoroughly blended. Stir in nuts and vanilla. Pour into prepared pan. Refrigerate until firm. Cut into squares.

If using a conventional thermometer, do not leave in oven during cooking.

Cinnamon-Sugar Nuts _____ 2 cups nuts

Total Cooking Time: 6 to 7 minutes

1 large egg white (about
   2 tablespoons)
2 cups (8 ounces) pecan
   halves
¼ cup firmly packed brown
   sugar
1 teaspoon cinnamon

Combine egg white and pecans in small bowl; mix until pecans are moistened. In another small bowl, combine brown sugar and cinnamon; mix well. Add to nuts; mix until coated. Pour into greased 9-inch microproof pie plate. Use COOK cycle and cook 6 to 7 minutes, or until coating is no longer glossy, stirring twice during cooking time. Let stand until cool. Store in airtight container.

Fairy Food ———————————————— 1 pound

Total Cooking Time: 17 to 20½ minutes

1 cup sugar
1 cup dark corn syrup
1 tablespoon vinegar
1 tablespoon baking soda
1 tablespoon shortening
1 pound semisweet dipping
   chocolate

Line 8-inch square baking dish with aluminum foil; butter generously; set aside.

In 2-quart glass measure or microproof bowl, combine sugar, corn syrup, and vinegar. Use COOK cycle and cook 5 minutes, stirring several times during cooking time. Continue to use COOK cycle and cook 8 to 10 minutes, or until mixture is thickened and microproof candy thermometer registers 300°F (or a small amount dropped in cold water separates into hard, brittle threads). Quickly stir in baking soda; blend well. Pour into prepared dish. Spread evenly with spoon or tip baking dish to cover bottom evenly. Let stand 1 hour, or until firm. Break hardened mixture into pieces; set aside.

Break up chocolate and place in 2-quart glass measure. Add shortening. Use COOK cycle and cook 4 to 5½ minutes, or until melted, stirring once during cooking. Dip hardened pieces in chocolate, covering completely. Place on waxed paper to cool. Store in refrigerator in an airtight container.

Chocolate Almond Bark ————————— 1½ pounds

Total Cooking Time: 9 to 10½ minutes

1 cup blanched whole
   almonds
1 teaspoon butter or
   margarine
1 pound semisweet or milk
   chocolate

Combine almonds and butter in 9-inch glass pie plate. Use COOK cycle and cook 5 to 6 minutes, or until almonds are golden, stirring twice during cooking time; set aside. Place chocolate in 2-quart glass measure. Use COOK cycle and cook 4 to 4½ minutes, or until melted. Stir in almonds. Pour onto waxed paper-lined baking sheet. Spread to desired thickness. Refrigerate until firm. Break into pieces to serve. Store in cool place.

Dry-Roasted Peanut Brittle _____ about 1 pound
Total Cooking Time: 12 to 13 minutes

1 cup sugar
½ cup light corn syrup
1¾ cups dry-roasted unsalted peanuts
1 tablespoon butter or margarine
1 teaspoon vanilla
1 teaspoon baking soda

Generously grease baking sheet. In 2-quart microproof bowl, combine sugar and corn syrup. Use COOK cycle and cook 6 minutes. Stir in peanuts with wooden spoon. Use COOK cycle and cook 6 to 7 minutes, or until mixture reaches 300°F on microproof candy thermometer (or a small amount separates into hard, brittle threads when dropped in cold water). Stir in butter and vanilla. Blend in baking soda; stir until mixture is light and foamy. Pour onto prepared sheet; spread quickly. As candy cools, stretch into thin sheet using buttered hands. Cool completely. Break into pieces and store in an airtight container.

Pumpkin Mousse _____ 8 servings
Total Cooking Time: 5½ to 6 minutes

½ cup evaporated milk
1 envelope unflavored gelatin
1 cup pumpkin pie filling
¼ cup firmly packed brown sugar
2 eggs, separated
½ teaspoon cinnamon
2 tablespoons sugar
1½ cups sweetened whipped cream or thawed frozen whipped topping, divided
Nutmeg

Combine milk and gelatin in 1-quart microproof bowl; let stand to soften gelatin. Stir in pumpkin pie filling, brown sugar, egg yolks, and cinnamon; beat until smooth. Use COOK cycle and cook 5½ to 6 minutes, or until mixture begins to boil, stirring every 2 minutes. Refrigerate until thickened.

In small mixing bowl, beat egg whites until frothy. Gradually beat in 2 tablespoons sugar until stiff peaks form. Fold 1 cup of whipped topping into cooled pumpkin mixture. Gently fold in egg whites. Spoon into 8 sherbet glasses. Refrigerate until chilled. Top with remaining whipped topping. Sprinkle with nutmeg.

Poached Pears _____ 8 servings
Total Cooking Time: 17 to 18 minutes

4 cups water, divided
3 tablespoons lemon juice
4 firm, ripe pears (6 to 8
  ounces each)
1 cup dry red wine
⅓ cup sugar
1 cinnamon stick
  Lemon peel strip

In mixing bowl, combine 3 cups of water and lemon juice. Peel pears; cut in half lengthwise; core. Place pears in lemon-water.
  In 2-quart microproof casserole, combine remaining water, wine, sugar, cinnamon, and lemon peel. Use COOK cycle and cook 7 minutes. Remove pears from water with slotted spoon; add to hot wine mixture. Turn pear halves to coat completely. Cover with waxed paper. Use COOK cycle and cook 10 to 11 minutes, or until pears are tender, turning pears twice during cooking time. Let stand, in syrup, until cool. Serve in sherbet dishes.

Cherries Jubilee _____ 6 to 8 servings
Total Cooking Time: 8¾ minutes

1 can (1 pound, 14 ounces)
  pitted bing cherries,
  ¼ cup juice reserved
1 jar (10 ounces) currant
  jelly
1 tablespoon lemon juice
1½ teaspoons cornstarch
1 teaspoon grated orange
  rind
¼ cup brandy

Combine reserved cherry juice, jelly, lemon juice, cornstarch, and orange rind in 2-quart glass measure or microproof bowl, stirring to dissolve cornstarch. Use COOK cycle and cook 4½ minutes, or until thickened, stirring once during cooking time. Add cherries. Use COOK cycle and cook 3½ minutes. Pour brandy into 1-cup glass measure. Use DEFROST cycle and cook 45 seconds. Ignite brandy and pour over cherry mixture. Serve, flaming, over vanilla ice cream or angel food cake.

If serving from a chafing dish, transfer cooked cherry mixture to dish before heating brandy. If serving over ice cream, spoon ice cream into serving dishes and place in freezer before sauce is cooked.

Marshmallow Crisp _____ 36 bars
Total Cooking Time: 4½ to 5 minutes

¼ cup butter or margarine
5 cups miniature (or 40 large) marshmallows
5 cups crispy rice cereal
1 cup chopped nuts

Lightly grease 12×7×2-inch baking dish; set aside. Place butter in 3-quart microproof casserole. Use COOK cycle and cook 1 minute, or until melted. Add marshmallows. Cover. Use COOK cycle and cook 3½ to 4 minutes, or until soft, stirring once during cooking time. Stir to combine marshmallows and butter. Add cereal and nuts; stir until thoroughly coated. Press warm mixture into prepared dish. Let stand until cool. Cut into bars.

Raisin-Nut Bars _____ 18 to 20 bars
Total Cooking Time: 18 to 20 minutes

1 cup raisins, chopped
½ cup apple juice
2 tablespoons sugar
1 teaspoon all-purpose flour
½ cup chopped nuts, divided
½ cup butter or margarine, room temperature
½ cup firmly packed brown sugar
1 teaspoon vanilla
1 teaspoon baking powder
¾ cup all-purpose flour
1½ cups quick-cooking oats

Combine raisins, apple juice, sugar, and the 1 teaspoon flour in 4-cup glass measure. Cover with plastic wrap. Use COOK cycle and cook 5 to 6 minutes, or until thickened, stirring once during cooking time. Stir in ¼ cup of nuts; set aside.

In mixing bowl, cream butter, brown sugar, and vanilla. Mix baking powder with ¾ cup flour; add to creamed mixture. Stir in oats and remaining nuts. Press half of the flour mixture into 8-inch round microproof baking dish. Use COOK cycle and cook 6 minutes, or until surface is no longer moist. Spread raisin mixture on top. Spoon remaining flour mixture over raisin filling; press lightly. Use COOK cycle and cook 7 to 8 minutes, or until no longer moist on top. Let stand in pan on heat-resistant counter top or breadboard until cool. Cut into squares.

Lemon Bars ——————————————— 16 bars
Total Cooking Time: 12 minutes

1 cup all-purpose flour
½ cup butter or margarine, room temperature
⅓ cup confectioners sugar
2 eggs
1 cup sugar
2 tablespoons flour
2 tablespoons lemon juice
1 teaspoon grated lemon rind
½ teaspoon baking powder
Confectioners sugar

Mix flour, butter, and ⅓ cup confectioners sugar until crumbly. Press into bottom of 8-inch square microproof pan. Use COOK cycle and cook 6 minutes. Combine remaining ingredients, except last addition of confectioners sugar; beat with electric mixer until smooth. Pour over baked crust. Use COOK cycle and cook 6 minutes, or until center tests done, rotating dish if bars are rising unevenly. Let stand, covered with waxed paper, 4 minutes. Remove waxed paper, cool, and cut into bars. Sprinkle with confectioners sugar.

Granola Nut Drops ——————————— 36 servings
Total Cooking Time: 3 to 4 minutes

1 package (6 ounces) semi-sweet chocolate pieces
1 tablespoon peanut butter
1½ cups granola with coconut and nuts
½ cup wheat flakes cereal
½ cup chopped dates
½ cup raisins

Combine chocolate and peanut butter in 2-quart glass measure. Use COOK cycle and cook 3 to 4 minutes, or until chocolate is melted. Stir until smooth. Add remaining ingredients and stir until thoroughly coated. Drop by teaspoonfuls onto waxed paper. Chill until firm.

Lemon Bars, Dry-Roasted Peanut Brittle (page 165)→

Chewy Coconut Bars ———————— 18 to 20 bars
Total Cooking Time: 11 minutes

½ cup butter or margarine
2 eggs
¾ cup firmly packed brown
    sugar
½ cup all-purpose flour
1 teaspoon baking powder
1 teaspoon vanilla
1 cup chopped nuts
1 cup flaked coconut
Confectioners sugar

Place butter in 1-cup glass measure. Use COOK cycle and cook 2 minutes, or until melted; set aside. In mixing bowl, beat eggs until light and fluffy. Add brown sugar, flour, baking powder, vanilla, and melted butter; blend thoroughly. Stir in nuts and coconut. Pour into 8-inch square microproof baking dish. Use COOK cycle and cook 9 minutes, rotating dish once during cooking time. Mixture will be moist, but will firm as it cools. Let stand on heat-resistant counter top or breadboard until cool. Sprinkle with confectioners sugar. Cut into squares.

Peanut Chocolate Sauce ———————— 1 cup
Total Cooking Time: 4 minutes

1 square (1 ounce) unsweetened
    baking chocolate
¼ cup milk
1 cup sugar
2 tablespoons butter or
    margarine
¼ teaspoon vanilla
1 cup chopped salted
    peanuts

In 4-cup glass measure, combine chocolate and milk. Use COOK cycle and cook 2 minutes, or until chocolate is melted; stir. Stir in sugar. Use COOK cycle and cook 2 minutes, or until mixture boils. Stir in butter and vanilla, until butter is melted. Stir in nuts. Serve warm or cold over ice cream or cake.

Applesauce ———————————————— 4 servings
Total Cooking Time: 6 minutes

4 tart cooking apples,
    cored and sliced
    (peeled, if desired)
1 tablespoon sugar
1 teaspoon cinnamon

Arrange apple slices in 1½-quart microproof baking dish. Mix sugar and cinnamon; sprinkle over apples. Cover. Use COOK cycle and cook 6 minutes. Transfer to blender or food processor; blend to desired consistency.

Caramel Sauce———————— 1 cup
Total Cooking Time: 4 to 5 minutes

½ pound (28) vanilla
   caramels
⅓ cup water
¼ cup chopped nuts

In 4-cup glass measure, combine caramels and water. Use COOK cycle and cook 4 to 5 minutes, or until melted. Stir until smooth. Stir in nuts. Serve over ice cream, cake, baked apples, or fruit cobblers.

Raspberry Sauce———————— ¾ cup
Total Cooking Time: 9 to 9½ minutes

1 package (10 ounces)
   frozen raspberries
2 teaspoons cornstarch
1 teaspoon lemon juice

Place frozen berries in 4-cup glass measure. Use DEFROST cycle and cook 3 to 3½ minutes, or until thawed. Drain juice, reserve. Combine cornstarch with 1 tablespoon of raspberry juice; mix to make a paste. Stir in remaining raspberry juice. Stir in berries. Use COOK cycle and cook 6 minutes, stirring every 1 minute. Stir in lemon juice. Chill before serving. Serve over ice cream, cheesecake, pudding, or butter cake.

Cranberry Sauce ———————— 2 cups
Total Cooking Time: 8 to 9 minutes

1 package (12 ounces)
   fresh cranberries
   (about 3 cups)
½ cup sugar
⅓ cup water
⅛ teaspoon almond extract

Combine all ingredients, except almond extract, in 2-quart microproof bowl. Cover with plastic wrap. Use COOK cycle and cook 8 to 9 minutes, or until berries pop. Stir in almond extract. Let stand until cool. Cover and refrigerate until ready to serve.

INDEX

(Recipe page appears in dark type when two or more pages are cited.)